Job Interview Ques

UNIX® SHELL PROGRAMMING
INTERVIEW QUESTIONS
YOU'LL MOST LIKELY BE ASKED

352
Interview Questions

UNIX® Shell Programming
Interview Questions
You'll Most Likely Be Asked

© 2021, By Vibrant Publishers, USA. All rights reserved. No part of this publication may be reproduced or distributed in any form or by any means, or stored in a database or retrieval system, without the prior permission of the publisher.

ISBN-10: 1-949395-02-2
ISBN-13: 978-1-949395-02-0

Library of Congress Control Number: 2011911708

This publication is designed to provide accurate and authoritative information in regard to the subject matter covered. The author has made every effort in the preparation of this book to ensure the accuracy of the information. However, information in this book is sold without warranty either expressed or implied. The Author or the Publisher will not be liable for any damages caused or alleged to be caused either directly or indirectly by this book.

Vibrant Publishers books are available at special quantity discount for sales promotions, or for use in corporate training programs. For more information please write to **bulkorders@vibrantpublishers.com**

Please email feedback / corrections (technical, grammatical or spelling) to **spellerrors@vibrantpublishers.com**

To access the complete catalogue of Vibrant Publishers, visit **www.vibrantpublishers.com**

Table of Contents

chapter 1	C Shell – Beginner	7
chapter 2	C Shell – Intermediate	15
chapter 3	C Shell – Advanced	29
chapter 4	Bash – Beginner	59
chapter 5	Bash – Intermediate	69
chapter 6	Bash – Advanced	83
chapter 7	Basics	103
chapter 8	Commands	107
chapter 9	Variables and Arrays	115
chapter 10	Special Shell Variables	121
chapter 11	Operators and Shell Substitutions	125
	HR Interview Questions	131
	Index	158

Dear Reader,

Thank you for purchasing **UNIX Shell Programming Interview Questions You'll Most Likely Be Asked.** We are committed to publishing books that are content-rich, concise and approachable enabling more readers to read and make the fullest use of them. We hope this book provides the most enriching learning experience as you prepare for your interview.

Should you have any questions or suggestions, feel free to email us at
reachus@vibrantpublishers.com

Thanks again for your purchase. Good luck with your interview!

— Vibrant Publishers Team

facebook.com/vibrantpublishers

UNIX **Shell Programming** Interview Questions

Review these typical interview questions and think about how you would answer them. Read the answers listed; you will find best possible answers along with strategies and suggestions.

www.vibrantpublishers.com

This page is intentionally left blank

Chapter 1

C Shell – Beginner

1: What must you do before you are able to run your new script for the first time by its name or with an alias?

Answer:

You must make it executable, that is to execute the command:

chmod +x scriptname

2: The following command is included in the *.login* script of a user:

alias whois ´grep \!^ /etc/passwd´

What will be the output, when the user issues the following?

who is guru

Answer:

If there is a defined user account named "*guru*", or the string guru is contained elsewhere in */etc/passwd* file, then the output will be the entry which contains the string "*guru*", otherwise, it will be an empty line.

3: If the condition If (-r *filename*)fails (returns false), what are the possible reasons?

Answer:

The possible reasons are:

a) filename is not readable by the owner of the process

b) filename does not exist

4: Which is the difference between the next two statements?

set var =99

@ var = 99

Answer:

Using the typical assignment form (set …), the value assigned in *var* is the string 99. Using the @, the value is the integer 99.

5: Given the code snippet:

@ n = 5

while ($n)

   # actions

…

end

What actions should be performed inside the loop, in order to get out of this loop?

Answer:

Any command that changes the value of variable *n*, for it to become 0 sometime. E.g., @ *n—*

C Shell – Beginner 9

6: What will the output of the following commands be? Explain.

set names =(Kathrin Chris Jacob)

shift names

echo $#names

Answer:

The output will be 2.

shift command gets rid of the first element of the array names. So, the *echo* command will display 2 as the number of elements of the array.

7: What does the command *rehash* do?

Answer:

Rehash recomputes the internal hash table for the PATH variable. If the new command resides in a directory not listed in PATH, add this directory to PATH, and then use rehash.

8: How could you ensure that a script will be run in *csh*?

Answer:

The first line of the script could be used to define the shell you want to use, as follows:

#!/bin/csh

This is sufficient to run the script in *csh*.

9: Given that *script1* is an executable C shell script situated in directory */home/myhomedir/project1/data/dir1*, use three ways to run it, explaining the pros and cons.

Answer:

   a) *cd/home/myhomedir/project1/data/dir1/script1*

(You should first *cd* to the directory path)

b) */home/myhomedir/project1/data/dir1/script1*

   (You should include the absolute directory path)

c) *script1* (shortest form, but it works only if the directory path is added to the PATH environment variable of the user)

10: What will be the value of the *sixrem* variable, after executing this command?

@ sixrem = $data[2] % 6

Answer:

The expression divides the value of second element of the data array by 6 and assigns the remainder of the division to the *sixrem* variable.

11: Name two ways to obtain the length of a string, giving a simple example for each one.

Answer:

The two ways to obtain the length of a string are:

a) Using the *wc* command:

   set string = "any string"

   @ ln = `echo $string | wc -c` -1

b) Using the *awk* function length:

   set string = "any string"

   set ln = `echo $string | awk '{print length($0)}'`

12: Create a script that displays a list of regular files from the current directory.

Answer:

```
#!/bin/csh -f
foreach i (*)
   if( -f $i ) then
      print $i
   endif
end
```

13: Describe in short, the word-completion feature of the *tcsh* shell.

Answer:

If you want word completion to work, whether on commands or filenames, you just need to type the beginning of the word and press the Tab key. The Shell will substitute the unfinished word with a complete one which is available in the input buffer and also adds a "/" to its end if it's a directory and a space if it's a word. The shell will check the buffer to identify whether the completed word is a word or a command, variable or filename. The buffer considers the first word in it and the words following {'|', '|&', ';', '&&', '||'} as a command. If the word starts with a $ it's a variable and everything else is a filename. If there's an empty line, it is completed as a filename.

14: In *tcsh*, how are the remaining choices (if any) listed whenever the word completion fails?

Answer:

The remaining choices (if any), are listed only if the shell variable *autolist* is set.

15: In *tcsh*, how do you disable filename substitution?

Answer:

noglob shell variable can be set to disable the filename substitution feature.

16: Compare the *sched tcsh* built-in command with the UNIX/Linux at command.

Answer:

These commands are similar but not the same. *sched* command runs directly from the shell, so it has access to shell variables and settings at command can run a scheduled command at exactly the specified time.

17: Schedule a *prompt* change at 10:55 as a reminder for an oncoming event.

Answer:

sched 10:55 set prompt = 'It \ 's time for the important meeting: >'

18: What is the impact of *-f* option in the first line of a *csh* script? (*#!/bin/csh*

versus

#!/bin/csh -f)

Answer:

When you add the *-f* option to *csh*, the shell will skip loading the startup files *.cshrc* and resources. It will also skip the hashing process. The shell will load quicker because of that.

19: How can you start a job in the background, and then terminate your login session, without terminating the background job?

Answer:

We can start a job in the background and then terminate our login session, without terminating the background job using "no hangup" command, *nohup:*

nohup command > output_file &

20: Which is the difference between

echo c{1,4,2,5,1}

and

echo [c]{1,4,2,5,1}?

Answer:

The first *echo* will display *c1 c4 c2 c5 c1*, while the second displays only *c1*.

21: Display the first and last arguments of a script, regardless of the number of arguments, and without a loop.

Answer:

my_var3 = $#argv

echomy_var1: $argv[$1]

echomy_last_var: $argv[$my_var3]

22: How will you set the 'search path' in *csv*?

Answer:

Search path in *csv* can be set as follows:

a) *setenv PATH"/myfolder1 /bin: /myfolder2 /myfile3"*

b) using list
   set path =(/myfolder1 /bin /myfolder2 /myfile3)

23: Create a tar archive into /home/user1/myarch.tar, including all files ending in .c, .h, .l, .y,.o and .cc and also the *Makefile* from two directories, ~/dir1 and ~/dir2.

Answer:

tar cvf /home/user1/myarch.tar ~/{dir1,dir2}/{Makefile,*.{c,h,l,o,y,cc}}

or

tar cvf /home/user1/myarch.tar ~/dir1/Makefile ~/dir1/*.[chloy] ~/dir1/*.cc ~/dir2/Makefile ~/dir2/*.[chloy] ~/dir2/*.cc

24: Your script must be executed with exactly two arguments, otherwise would be terminated. Write a code to implement these checks.

Answer:

if ($#argv <> 2) then
echo "Usage: $0 arg1 arg2"
echo "You must give exactly two parameters"
exit 20
endif

25: Write a pipeline that reads from the *j-th* line up to the *k-th* line of a text file, without using *awk*.

Answer:

set total = `cat textfile | wc -l`
set j = 10
set k = 18
@ count = $k - $j
head -$k textfile | tail -$count

Chapter 2

C Shell – Intermediate

26: Explain the following commands:

set names = *(John Kathrin Chris Jacob)*

set names = *($names[1-2] Angela $names[3-])*

Answer:

First command creates an array named *names* with the four names as its elements.

Second command adds name *Angela* between *Kathrin* and *Chris*.

27: How could you move cursor to specified coordinates on screen? (*tcsh*)

Answer:

We can move the cursor to specified coordinates on the screen using the following code: *echotc cm column row*

www.vibrantpublishers.com

28: What is the result of this loop?

foreach i ([A-Z]) ? mv $i $i.csh ? end*

Answer:

The loop renames all files that begin with a capital letter, adding the "extension" .csh.

29: Assuming there is a label cleanup somewhere in a script, explain the command *onintr cleanup*.

Answer:

The script will branch to label "cleanup" if it catches an interrupt signal.

30: Is there a way to repeat a command for a predefined number of times, without using a counter-controlled loop?

Answer:

We can repeat a command for a predefined number of times, without using a counter-controlled loop using the *repeat* command, e.g.,

repeat 5 ls >> listings

31: *csh* and *tcsh* both support the filename and command completion feature. But the feature works differently in *csh* than in *tcsh*. Name the differences.

Answer:

When you use *tcsh*, the commands and filenames are automatically completed when you press the Tab key.

When you use *csh*, you have to set the *filec* variable for word completion to work. In *csh*, the Esc key has to be pressed for word completion.

32: Name the special login files for *csh* and *tcsh* in the order used by each shell.

Answer:

If the command is executed from the *("/etc/csh.cshrc&/etc/csh.login")* system files, the login shell will be started. It will run the commands given in the files present in the home directory of the user.

a) *~/.cshrc* or *~/.tcshrc*: During shell startup, it gets executed for each instance of the shell. If *~/.cshrcs* present, '*tcsh*' uses this file else executes '*~/.tcshrc*'

b) *~/.login*: at login it is executed after *.cshrcby* login shell

c) *~/.cshdirs*: After .login (*tcsh*), it is executed by login shell

33: What do the following lines do? Explain the differences.

ls > filename

ls >! Filename

Answer:

In both forms, the output of *ls* command is redirected to filename. If filename does not exist, it will be created, otherwise it will be truncated. When the first form is used, if shell parameter *noclobber* is set and filename is an existing file, an error results. The '!' in the second form is used to suppress that check.

34: You can run a script by its name, using an alias or using source. Explain the differences in using each of the three methods. When is it suitable to use each method?

Answer:

A script executed by name is not run in current process (a child process is created to run the script), so this method is suitable to be used only if the environment variables and globally defined aliases (in *$HOME/.cshrc*) should be known to the script.

The method that executes a script using an alias is a variant of executing the script by name. In addition, if the alias is defined from shell prompt, it applies only to the current process. To make the alias global, you must define it in *$HOME/.cshrc*, but be careful to keep the number of aliases included there to a relatively small number.

With the third method, the script runs in the current process, thus, any aliases defined in the current process will be known to your script.

35: How could you override a defined alias? Give a simple example.

Answer:

You can define alias with the "\" or backslash. To create an alias of a script, use the "\" before its name and give the filename. Within this, you can customize how your overridden alias should function. For example,

mymethod<myfilename>

@*varname*++

End

36: You plan to write a script that will process the file passed to it as the only argument on the command line. So, your script must accept at least one argument and this single or first argument must be an existing file. Write the necessary checks, displaying the appropriate messages.

Answer:

The following piece of code should be added to your code before

C Shell – Intermediate

you start processing the file content.

```
#!/bin/csh
  if ( $#argv == 0 ) then
    echo Error: A file name must be supplied as argument
    exit 10
  else if ( ! -e $1 ) then
    echo Error:  $1 is not an existing file
    exit  11
  endif
```

After this, you can add the code to process the content of the file.

37: Write a code excerpt that processes (here, just displays) the elements of an array, from the first one to the last one.

Answer:

```
set myarray = (value1, value2, value3, value4, value5)
set i = 1
while ( $#myarray > 0 )
   echo "$i array's element is: $myarray[1]"
   shift myarray
   @ i++
end
```

or,

```
set myarray = (value1, value2, value3, value4, value5)
set i = 1
foreach val ( $myarray[*] )
   echo "$i array's element is: $val"
   @ i++
```

www.vibrantpublishers.com

End

38: Complete the last echo command with a descriptive message in the following script. In other words, explain the value of *pct* variable.

#!/bin/csh

set duout = (`du -sk ~`)

@ dir_size = $duout[1]

set dfout = (`df -k | grep /home`)

@ home_size = $dfout[2]

*@ pct = $dir_size * 100 / $home_size*

echo " .... $pct ......"

Answer:

echo "Your home directory takes *$pct % of /home filesystem*"

39: Extract just the mode of a given file, using two different ways.

Answer:

The mode of a given file can be extracted in the following ways:
   a) *set file_mode = `ls -l filename | tail -1 | cut -f1 -d" " | cut -c2-`*
   b) *set file_mode = `ls -l filename | awk ' /^-/ {print substr($1,2)}'`*

40: Which is the output of the following excerpt?

netstat -an | awk '/SHED/ {split($4,c,"."); print "Connection to " c[4] " from " $5}' | sort -nt" " -k 3

Answer:

Lines in the format "Connection to *port_number* from

IP_Address", for each established connection, sorted by *port_number*.

41: Find the position of a substring in a given string. Display a message if the string does not contain this substring.

Answer:

set string = "any string"

set sub = "str"

set pos = `echo $string | awk -v s=$sub '{print index($0,s)}'`

if ($pos == 0) then

   echo "$string does not contain the substring $sub"

else

   echo "$sub first occurrence in $string starts in position $pos"

endif

42: Change the case of a string.

Answer:

set string = "C Shell Programming"

set ustring = `echo $string | awk '{print toupper($0)}'` # = "C SHELL PROGRAMMING"

set lstring = `echo $string | awk '{print tolower($0)}'` # = "c shell programming"

43: Assume that in a script the value of a variable *limt* becomes equal to 92.1. Display the message:

Upper limit 92.10% in *yoursystem*

Answer:

if [$limt == 92.10]

then

printf "Upper limit 92.10%% in $HOSTNAME"

fi

44: Suppose a script contains the following snippet.

set fl = /home/dbuser5/reports/fs_report1.txt

echo $fl:e

echo $fl:r

echo $fl:t

echo $fl:h

What do you expect to be displayed?

Answer:

txt

fs_report1

fs_report1.txt

/home/dbuser5/reports

45: Create a script that converts the filenames from current directory to lower case letters.

Answer:

#!/bin/csh -f

foreachmy_old_file1 (`ls`)

  setmy_new_file1 = `echo $my_old_file1 | tr '[A-Z]' '[a-z]'`

  if ("$my_new_file1" == "$my_old_file1") then

    continue

  endif

  mv $ my_old_file1 $my_new_file1

end

46: Name some basic differences between *csh* and *tcsh*.

Answer:

tcsh includes a command-line editor, file name and command completion features, and enhanced job control, in comparison with the Berkeley *csh*.

47: Compare the *tcsh* shell variables *correct* and *autocorrect*.

Answer:

Autocorrect can be set to correct the word to be completed before any completion attempt. *Correct* can be set to *'cmd'* to correct command names or to 'all' to correct the entire line, each time return is hit.

48: What is the purpose of the special alias shell?

Answer:

The shell special alias can be set to specify an interpreter other than the shell itself.

49: Which is the method to bind the keys to the standard *vi* or *emacs* bindings?

Answer:

Shell's built-in command is *bindkey*. Its -e option binds all keys to standard *emacs* bindings, while -v option binds to standard *vi* bindings.

50: Which is the purpose of shell's variable *color*?

Answer:

Shell's variable *color*, if set, enables color display for the built in *ls-F* and it passes *--color=auto* to *ls*.

51: Set your prompt to display *username@hostname: pwd>*

Answer:

It can be done as follows:

set prompt = "%n@%m: %/ >"

52: How can you start (from shell prompt) 2 commands "in the background", ensuring that the second command will start after the completion of the first one?

Answer:

It can be done as follows:

(command1 ;command 2) &

53: Write a script to display a sorted listing of the unique words in a text file.

Answer:

It can be done as follows:

#!/bin/csh

set txt_file = text_file_name

tr -s ' ' < $txt_file | tr ' ' '\n' | sort | uniq

54: Display the value of your PATH variable with each path in a separate line.

Answer:

It can be done as follows:

echo $PATH | tr ':' '\n' | sort

55: Why the inclusion of a dot (.) in a search path is not a good practice?

Answer:

The current working directory may be a world writable directory (*like /tmp*). World writable directories must not be included in the PATH variable due to security reasons. It may also cause problems in the execution of commands, if the current directory contains executable files - the names of which match reserved words (standard commands, etc). So, the inclusion of a dot (.) in a search path is not a good practice.

56: Explain the logical expression @ x = ($n < 5$ || $20 <= \$n$) and then also write the negation of this expression.

Answer:

a) *x= false when n={5 to 19}*

   else,

   x=true

b) Negation of *x: (y)*

   @ y = (!($n < 5$ || $20 <= \$n$))

57: What are the differences between the two commands given below and when can we use both of them?

csh-x my_new_script

csh-v my_new_script

Answer:

csh −x my_new_script

    a) After variable substitution, it displays the command line

    b) Finds and locates the errors in variable substitution

    csh −v my_new_script

    a) Before variable substitution, it displays the command line

    b) Finds the line where the script is failing

58: Explain this small script:

#!/bin/csh

foreach dfile (/home/users/project1/*)

  if (-z $dfile || $dfile == "core") then

    rm $dfile

  endif

end

Answer:

This script will delete zero length files and dumped core files from the specified directory.

59: A script prompts the user to type in something, using the following syntax:

echo -n "Enter some input ->"

set IN = $<

What would happen if the user had typed? *A B C D E*

Correct your syntax to avoid the possible problems.

Answer:

The shell replaces the $ < with the user input, that is:

set IN = A B C D E

and then executes that command. This set command, however, will assign the value *A* to the *IN* variable, a *C* to the *B* variable, an *E* to the *D* variable, so after the execution of the above command, in the script there will be 3 variables, instead of one (*IN*).

The solution is to use $< in quotes (double):

set IN = "$<"

Thus, when the user inputs the string *A B C D E*, the shell will have the following command to execute:

set IN = "A B C D E"

and it will assign the quoted string to the *IN* variable.

This page is intentionally left blank

facebook.com/vibrantpublishers

Chapter 3

C Shell – Advanced

60: Explain local vs environment variables.

Answer:

Local variables are exclusive to the shell in which they are set. Environment variables are available to all subshells within the environment. While local variables are created inside specific shells, the environment variables are set in the *.cshrc* file or *.login* file. Environment variables inherit the value of its parent. While the child can change the value set by the parent, the parent cannot change the value of its child.

61: Explain search path.

Answer:

The search path contains the path of various executables to search for shell executables when the shell is unable to identify a particular command. It is set as the environment variable in the prompt. You can change the default search path to a custom one and add multiple search paths where you have stored different executables with scripts. You can set and view the search path using the *path* system variable.

62: Explain Globbing.

Answer:

Globbing lets you search for a set of files or directories using a wildcard. When you are searching for a file or directory and you are not sure of its exact name, you can use a wildcard to search. Globbing expands the wildcard possibilities to bring you the list of files and directories based on the regular expression that depicts the name.

63: Fix the following switch statement, explaining your corrections.

switch ($argv[$i])

　case quit: breaksw

　case list: ls

　　breaksw

　case delete:

　case erase:

　　@ k = $i

　　rm $argv[$k]

　　breaksw

endsw

Answer:

switch ($argv[$i])

  case quit:

    breaksw # the commands for a particular case

      # MUST NOT be on the same line

  case list:

    ls # same as above

    breaksw

  case delete:

  case erase:

    @ k = $i + 1 # the value of $argv[$i] here is "erase"

      # a logical syntax would be script erase filename,

      # in order to erase the second argument.

    rm $argv[$k]

    breaksw

endsw

64: Name some basic differences between *bash* and *csh* syntax and/or features.

Answer:

The basic differences between *bash* and *csh* are:

  a) *Bash* shell has functions, C shell does not have

  b) *Bash* shell assigns values to variables using the assign operator *(variable=value)*; C shell uses set command *(set variable = value)*

  c) *Bash* shell has more advanced command substitution than C shell

  d) *Bash* shell has advanced file handling mechanisms; *csh* itself has no file handling capabilities

65: Suggest a way to overcome lack of functions in C shells.

Answer:

A way to overcome lack of functions is using a "clever" combination of alias and scripts. E.g.:

alias holder ' source ~$USER/.tsch/holder_func'

where the script *holder_func* contains the code to execute.

66: From /tmp directory, issue (cd ; pwd) ; pwd. Explain the performed actions and the output.

Answer:

cd returns user to his home directory, so the first *pwd* displays the home directory. But, since parenthesized commands are always executed in a subshell, second *pwd* displays /tmp, leaving the user where he was.

67: Write a code excerpt that prompts for a filename, reads the user input, checks if this is a regular file and if so, stores it in an array for further processing. The procedure must be repeated until the user hits the Enter key.

Answer:

#!/bin/csh

set i = 1

set fl = anything

while ($fl)

  echo -n "Give a filename ->"

  set fl = $<

  if ($fl = "") then

    break

facebook.com/vibrantpublishers

C Shell – Advanced

```
        endif
        if( ! -f $fl ) then
            continue
        endif
        set $files[$i] = $fl
        @ i++
end
echo "Number of files: $#files"
echo "Files are: $files[*]"
```

68: Use *awk* mathematical functions to calculate the area of a circle (area= PI*rad2)

Answer:

alias mathcalc ' awk "BEGIN{ print \! }" '*

set rad = 1.3

set circle_area = `mathcalc atan2(0,-1)*${rad}*${rad}`

Explanation: The *alias* defines a kind of mathematical calculator called *mathcalc*, which uses the "one-liner" *awk* to perform calculations (limited to the set of mathematical functions available in *awk*). Then, this calculator is used to calculate the circle's area. It uses the arctangent function *atan2* that evaluates PI.

69: Use *awk* in order to split an entry from /etc/passwd file into an array, replacing the password field with the string "*secret*".

Answer:

set user = username

set entry = `grep ^$user: /etc/passwd | awk' {$2 = "secret";
split($0,a,":"); for (i=1; i<=7; i++) print a[i]}'`

70: Explain the following snippet.

set ports = (`netstat -an | awk '/SHED/ {split($4,c,".");  print c[4]}'`)

set remaddrs = (`netstat -an | awk '/SHED/ print $5}'`)

@ i = 1

foreach port ($ports[*])

set service = `grep $port /etc/services | cut -f1 -d' '`

echo "$service connection established from $remaddrs[$i]"

@ i++

end

Answer:

It creates an array that holds the port numbers used for each established network connection and a second array that holds the corresponding remote IP Addresses. Then, using a *foreach* loop, "resolves" the port numbers to service names, and displays a descriptive message in the form "*Service_name* connection established from *Remote_IP_Address*" for each connection.

71: Name the available ways (with examples) to replace any occurrence of a substring with another substring in a string.

Answer:

The available ways to replace any occurrence of a substring with another substring in a string are:

a) Using *sed*:

   set sedstring = `echo $text | sed 's/search_string/replacement/g'`

b) Using *awk*:

   set awkstring = `echo $string | awk -v s1="$search" -v s2="$substitute" '{gsub(s1,s2); print $0}'`

c) Using editing modifiers: (limited use)

set text = "now is the time for all good men"

echo $text:gs/o/O/

72: Write a snippet to categorize the files from a directory, based on their extension (for simplicity, take care only for .c, .o, .txt, and .png files). Create an array for each extension, containing the filenames. Finally, display the number of files for each extension.

Answer:

#!/bin/csh

set dir = /home/~ # the directory path

foreach fl ($dir/*)

    switch ($fl)

        case *.c:

            set cfiles = ($cfiles[*] $fl)

            breaksw

        case*.o:

            set ofiles = (ofiles[*] $fl)

            breaksw

        case *.txt:

            set txtfiles = (txtfiles[*] $fl)

            breaksw

        case *.png:

            set pngfiles = (pngfiles[*] $fl)

            breaksw

        default:

>   breaksw
>   endsw
> end

echo "There are $#cfiles .c files, $#ofiles .o files, $#txtfiles txt files and $#pngfiles .png files in directory $dir"

73: Write a script that will display a menu of choices to the user. The menu should be displayed over and over, until the user will select the specific "exit" option. The script should give to the user the following options:

   a) rename a file

   b) display the contents of the file

   c) display the first and the last line of the file

   d) exit (or quit) the script

All the four choices (except exit) will ask for a filename and the script should check if that file exists or not. Is it possible to create a function to achieve this purpose?

Answer:

No, there is no safe way to return a variable's value, if it is defined in a child script, to its parent. The script goes as follows:

#!/bin/csh -f

set ans = 0

while ($ans != 4)

echo " MENU"

echo "================"

echo "1 Rename a file"

echo "2 View a file's contents"

echo "3 Examine 1st and last lines of a file"

```
echo "4 Quit - number 4 is the only acceptable choice"
echo ""
echo "Make your choice ->"
set ans = $<
switch ($ans)
   case [1Rr]:
      echo "Enter a filename ->"
      set fl = $<
      if ( ! -f "$fl" ) then
         echo "You must enter an existing file, try again..."
         breaksw
      endif
      mv $fl ${fl}.bak
      echo "Moving $fl to ${fl}.bak"
      breaksw
   case [2Vv]:
      echo "Enter a filename ->"
      set fl = $<
      if ( ! -f "$fl" ) then
         echo "You must enter an existing file, try again..."
         breaksw
      endif
      cat $fl
      breaksw
   case [3Ee]:
      echo "Enter a filename ->"
      set fl = $<
```

```
    if ( ! -f "$fl" ) then
        echo "You must enter an existing file, try again..."
        breaksw
    endif
    echo "First line:"
    head -1 $fl
    echo "Last line:"
    tail -1 $fl
    breaksw
  case 4:
    exit
  default:
echo "Only valid choices are the displayed numbers or the first letter of each choice, except the last one"
breaksw
endsw
end
```

74: Create a script that will be run automatically when the user logs into the system, and send a mail message to the user, if the total number of aliases on his .cshrc file are greater than a threshold (let's say 40).

Answer:

```
#!/bin/csh -f
set thres = 40
set total = `grep ^alias $HOME/.cshrc | wc -l`
if ($ total > $ thres ) then
```

C Shell – Advanced

mail -s "Too many aliases on your login scripts!!" $USER<< EOF

Dear user $USER

WARNING: Your defined aliases on your .cshrc are more than the allowed upper limit ($thres)

Please do the necessary changes to lower their number.

System Administrator

EOF

Endif

75: Display the filenames and permissions of each file in your current directory.

Answer:

set files = (`ls -l | grep -v ^total | tr -s ' ' | cut -f9 -d' '`)

set perms = (`ls -l | grep -v ^total | tr -s ' ' | cut -f1 -d' ' | cut -c2- `)

echo " FILE PERMISSIONS LIST "

echo " ===================="

set tot = $#files[*]

set count = 1

foreach fl ($files[*])

   echo "$fl \t $perms[$count]"

   @ count++

End

76: Create a script that creates a list of all file systems (mount points) on the current system and the current percent used.

Answer:

set fs = (`df | grep -v ^Filesystem | tr -s ' ' | cut -f5 -d' '`)

set pcts = (`df | grep -v ^Filesystem | tr -s ' ' | cut -f4 -d' '`)

```
set count = $#fs[*]
set i = 1
while ($i <= $count)
   echo "File system $fs[$i]  is $pct[$i} used"
   @ i++
End
```

77: **Explain the following script and suggest any enhancements.**

```
if ( -z "$1" )
then
   echo "Usage: `basename $0` filename"
   exit 20
fi
Username=guru
pword=/home/guru/password.file
Password=`cat $pword`
Filename=`basename $1`
Server="Servername"
Directory="dirpath"
ftp -n $Server <<EOF
user $Username $Password
binary
bell
cd $Directory
put $Filename
bye
EOF
```

C Shell – Advanced

exit 0

Answer:

The script checks if there is one argument in the command line. It starts an ftp session to a server, and using a "here" document, passes to it some ftp commands: username and password for that user, which is read from a file. During the session, it changes the directory and transfers a file to the remote server.

Suggestions: Security is the most important point with this script. It uses ftp (it would be better to use a secure equivalent, like sftp), and the password is stored in a text file in plain text!!!! It would be better to use the available encryption / decryption tools (like the standard crypt function).

The other point is the flexibility: All parameters are hard coded into the script. It would be better to ask them from the user during script's execution.

78: Use the *bc* calculator in order to do a variable comparison involving floating-point numbers. Write your example as part of an if conditional statement.

Answer:

set var1 = 0.4

if (`echo "if ( ${var1} <= 1.1 ) 1" | bc`) then

   <statements when $var1 is less than or equal to 1.1>

Endif

79: Write a while loop using a floating-point comparison statement as the loop condition (and loop control).

Answer:

set curvalue = 1.678*10^03

set upper = 1289.56

while (`echo "if ( $curvalue <= $upper) 1" | bc`)

  <statements when $curvalue <= 1289.56>

End

80: If there is no simple file reading facility in the C-shell, what could you use to tide this over?

Answer:

A combination of *awk* and shell loops is a work around as there is no simple file reading facility in the C-shell.

81: Extract the n-th line of a text file and assign it in a variable.

Answer:

set text = `awk -v ln=$j '{if (NR==ln) print $0}' textfile`

where variable *j* defines the n-th line.

82: Assuming that *input_file* is a text file with space-separated fields, what will be the value of *ncol* when the following command will be executed?

setncol = `awk '{if (FNR==1) print NF}' input_file`

Answer:

The number of fields in the first line of this file will be set as the value for "*ncol*" since

  a) FNR and NF are variables in '*awk*'

  b) Number of records read, will be assigned to "FNR"

  c) Number of fields in the record will be assigned to NF

C Shell – Advanced 43

83: Find the minimum of the integer numbers that are stored in an array.

Answer:

set array = (4, -2, 5, 8, 13, 1)

set array_org = ($array[*]) # create a clone, to preserve the original numbers

set min = $array[1]

while ($#array > 0) # if there is at least one element

  if ($min > $array[1]) then

    set min = $array[1]

  endif

  shift array # discards the first element of the array

end

echo "The original numbers are: $array_org[*]"

echo "The minimum number is: $min"

84: Explain the following block of commands:

foreach luser (`who | cut -f1 -d' ' | uniq`)

  if(-f /allfiles/$luser.msg) then

    mail $luser < $luser.msg

    echo "Message sent to $luser"

  else

    mail $luser << END

    Dear $luser,

    No message file has been created for you.

    Please check your settings

    END

endif

end

Answer:

The *luser* variable takes as value the username of each logged in user in the system (unique names, if some users have more than one login sessions). Inside the loop it checks if a "personalized" message file exists for each user, which is named in the format "*username.msg*". If so, it sends that file to the user mailbox. If not, it creates a message using the "here document" and it sends it to the user, informing him about the nonexistence of the file he is waiting for.

85: The C shell provides one way to read a line:

set VAR = $<

Which is the limitation of this syntax?

Answer:

This command always reads from standard input. $ < is only STDIN, and cannot change for the duration of the script.

86: Explain the following snippet.

foreachmy_line ("`cat /etc1/my_passwd`")

　setmy_line = "$my_line:gas1/ /_/"

　setmy_line = "$my_line:gas1/:/ /"

　setargv = ($my_line)

　setmy_name1 = $1

　setmy_name2 = "$5:gas1/_/ /"

　echo $my_name2

end

C Shell – Advanced

Answer:

It is a possible workaround in order to read a file line by line. In each loop iteration, the line variable takes the next line from the /etc1/my_passwd file (note the double quotes around the `cat/etc1/my_passwd`), and then, using variable modifiers, the script replaces first the spaces with underscores and then the colon (:) with spaces. Then it sets the positional parameters to the fields of the line, it replaces again the underscores with a space, and displays the comments field.

87: Fix any syntax or logical error in the following script.

This script creates a list of the subdirectories in a path
#!/bin/csh

echo "Subdirectories in $DirPath"

cd $DirPath

foreach file (*)

   if (-e $file) then

     echo $file

   endif

end

Answer:

  a) The line #!/bin/csh must be the FIRST in the script

  b) The *DirPath* variable is not set, so, the *cd $DirPath* command changes to the user's home directory (*cd*)

  c) The test (-e $file) checks if the value of file variable exists, not if it is a directory. It must be: (-d "$file")

  d) It is safer to use double quotes around the variable substitution expressions, e.g. "$file"

The correct script is:

```
#!/bin/csh
# This script creates a list of the subdirectories in a path
set DirPath = "/home/user1/mydir"
echo "Subdirectories in $DirPath"
cd "$DirPath"
foreach file (*)
  if ( -d "$file" ) then
    echo "$file"
  endif
end
```

88: Explain this script.

```
#!/bin/csh
echo "FILES # LINES SIZE"
cd
foreach FL (*)
  if ( -f "$FL" ) then
    set count = `cat "$FL" | wc -l `
    set size = `ls -l "$FL" | tr -s ' ' | cut -f5 -d' ' `
    echo "$FL$count $size"
  endif
end
```

Answer:

This script creates a report for all regular files in user's home directory, displaying the name of the file (1st column), the number of lines contained into the file (2nd column) and its size (3rd column).

C Shell – Advanced

89: Are there any differences between the next two commands?

set lines = `cat filename | wc -l`

set lines = (`wc -l filename`)

Answer:

In the first command, the output is just the lines count (only the number), while in the second one the output is the lines count and the filename (that is why the parentheses are necessary).

In the first statement, the used *cat* command decelerates the execution, so it will be slower than the second one.

90: Explain the following code block.

set string = "This is a string that contains the substring str 3 times"

set sub = "str"

set pos = (1)

set origstr = "$string"

while ($pos[1] > 0)

  set pos = `echo $string | awk -v s=$sub '{ps = index($0,s); print ps, substr($0,ps)}'`

  if ($pos[1] > 0) then

    set positions = ($positions[*] $pos[1])

    set string = "$pos[2-]"

  endif

end

echo "Substring $sub found in $#positions:"

echo $positions[*]

Answer:

It uses the *awk* functions *index* and *substr* in combination with a while loop in order to find every occurrence of a given substring in a string and displays the positions of them. Each time inside the loop the *awk* returns as a pair of one position and the remaining substring, and this pair is stored in an array. In the next iteration of the loop, the previously extracted substring is used, until the *awk* function index returns 0, meaning that the substring could not be located.

91: Suppose that you have a contacts file in the format (no headers line):

Name, Surname, Street, City, State, email, Telephone

Explain the following excerpt.

#!/bin/csh

foreach record ("`cat contacts`")
  set record = "$record:gas/ /_/"
  set record = "$record:gas/\,/ /"
  set argv = "$record"
  set name = "$1:gas/_/ /"
  set surname = "$2:gas/_/ /"
  set street = "$3:gas/_/ /"
  set city = "$4:gas/_/ /"
  set state = "$5"
  set email = "$6:gas/_/ /"
  set tel = "$7:gas/_/ /"
  echo "RR Name: $2 $1" >> ${5}.contacts
  echo " $3 $4" >> ${5}.contacts
  echo " $6 " >> ${5}.contacts

C Shell – Advanced 49

```
        echo "              $7 " >> ${5}.contacts
end
```

Answer:

This script creates one contacts file of each state, named *state.contacts*. It processes the original contacts file, line by line, replacing the spaces with underscores and then the commas with spaces. Then it sets the positional parameters to the fields of each line, sets 7 variables (one for each field), and echoes these variables in 4 lines, appending them to the appropriate file for that state.

92: Which is the valid syntax of *getopt* command in a C shell?

Answer:

The valid syntax is:

set argv=`getopt OptionString $*`

93: Explain in short, the following script.

```
#!/bin/csh
set OUTPUT_FILE=""
set DO_LONG=""
set argv="`getopt "hlo:" $*`"
if ( $status != 0 ) then
    echo "Usage: $0 [-l] [-o outputfile] [path ...]"
    exit 1
endif
while ( "$1" != "--" )
    switch($1)
        case "-h":
```

www.vibrantpublishers.com

```
    echo "Usage: $0 [-l] [-o outputfile] [path ...]"
    exit 1
  case "-o":
    set OUTPUT_FILE="$2"
    shift
    breaksw
  case "-l":
    set DO_LONG="-l"
    breaksw
  endsw
  shift
end
shift
if ( "$OUTPUT_FILE" == "" ) then
  ls $DO_LONG $*
else
  ls $DO_LONG $* > $OUTPUT_FILE
endif
```

Answer:

This script uses *getopt* command that processes the entire argument list at once. If the argument list matches, *getopt* canonicalizes (reorders in the typical way used by UNIX commands) the argument list, putting the flags and their optional arguments prior to any non-flag arguments, adding a single trailing "--" argument to indicate that there are no more flags to process.

In case of *-h* option, the script displays a *"usage"* message and terminates. In case of *-o* option, the script sets the OUTPUT_FILE

C Shell – Advanced 51

variable to the argument that follows. In case of -l option, the script sets the DO_LONG variable to -l. The shift command that follows the while loop removes trailing --.

The script runs ls $* (where $* are the remaining arguments), if no option was used; it runs ls -l $* command, if -l option was used and ls -l $* command, redirecting the output to OUTPUT_FILE file, if -o file was used.

94: Write a script which calculates the min, max and average of a set of floating-point numbers, stored in an array.

Answer:

set array = (5, 10, 2, 13, 0.2345)

foreach num ($array[*])

   echo $num >> nums_file

end

awk '{if(min==""){min=max=$1}; if($1>max) {max=$1}; if($1< min) {min=$1}; total+=$1; count+=1} END {print "Average is: "total/count, "Min is: "min, "Max is: "max}' nums_file

95: You have an input data file with a symmetrical schema (the same number of fields in each record) where the first line contains the headings of the fields. You want to extract the 3rd column (field) of the actual data records, that is, of each record except the headers line (1st line) and any comment lines (assume that they begin with # or *). Give a solution and explain it in short.

Answer:

set cn = 3

set ncols = `awk '{FNR == 1 {print NF}' input_file `

if ($cn <= $ncols) then

   set col$cn = ` awk -v i=$cn '$0 !~ /^[#*]/ && FNR != 1 { print $i }' input_file`

else

   echo "The column number must be in the range 1 to $ncols"

endif

The variable *ncols* contains the total number of columns in each record. The if structure is used to avoid the case where the position number of the requested column is greater than the total number of columns. *col3* will be an array of the values of the third column.

96: Suppose that *input_file* is a tabular data file with an asymmetric schema, that is, each record (line) may have different number of fields, and that the first 3 lines describe the used schema. Explain the following excerpt.

set cn = 3

set ccounts = `awk '{FNR > 3 {print NF}' input_file `

set ccounts1 = ($ccounts[*])

set ccounts2 = ($ccounts[*])

set mincn = $ccounts[1]

while ($ccounts1 > 0)

  if($mincn > $ccounts1[1]) then

    set mincn = $ccounts1[1]

  endif

  shift ccounts1

end

set maxcn = $ccounts2[1]

C Shell – Advanced 53

while ($ccounts2 > 0)

  if ($maxcn < $ccounts2[1]) then

    set maxcn = $ccounts2[1]

  endif

  shift ccounts2

end

if ($cn <= $maxcn) then

set col$cn = ` awk -v i=$cn -v minc=$mincn 'FNR > 3 { (FN < minc ) ? print FN "null" : print $i }' input_file`

else

  echo "The column number must be in the range $mincn to $maxcn"

endif

Answer:

This script extracts the content of a column from an asymmetric data file:

The *cn* variable holds the column to be extracted. The *ccounts* array holds the number of fields of all actual data records (*FNR>* 3). The arrays *ccounts1* and *ccounts2* are duplicates of the *ccount* array, used to calculate the minimum and maximum numbers from the array *ccounts*. We use these temporary arrays in order to preserve the original array to use it later. The first while loop calculates the minimum value and the second the maximum value. A *shift* command in each loop's iteration, discards the first element of the array. The if statement then checks if the number of the requested column (field) is less than the maximum number, and if so, the *awk* command prints the content of this column if there are any (*FN >= minc*), or the string "*FNnull*", otherwise. If the number of the requested column is greater than the maximum number, the script displays a message.

97: Suppose you have a data file but its internal format does not remain consistent. You want to extract two columns from this file, but you don't know the order of the columns, know only their headers: Name, and email.
Write the script that will achieve these tasks.

Answer:

#!/bin/csh -f

set fl = filename

set namepos = `head -1 "$fl" | awk '{split($0,a) ; for ( j in a ) { if (a[j] = "Name") {print j}}}' `

set mailpos = `head -1 "$fl" | awk '{split($0,a) ; for ( j in a ) { if (a[j] = "email") {print j}}}' `

foreach line ("`cat $fl`")

  set line = "$line:gas/ /_/"

  set argv = "$line"

  set name = "$argv[$namepos]"

  set name = "$name:gas/_/ /"

  set names = ($names[*] "$name")

  set mail = "$argv[$mailpos]"

  set mails = ($mails[*] "$mail")

end

98: Create a script to read a textfile line by line, to the end of the file. Do not use *awk*.

Answer:

```
set inputfile = textfile
set total = `cat $inputfile | wc -l`
@ count = 1

while ($count <= $total )
  if ($count == 1 )
    then
      set record = "`head $count $inputfile`"
      @ count++
    else
      set record = "`head -$count $inputfile | tail -$1`"
      @ count++
    endif
  <more commands to process the record>
End
```

99: What is a limitation in options handling in C shells?

Answer:

There is no equivalent to *getopts* bash built-in in C shells. The only way to handle command line options is the command *getopt*. This command processes the entire arguments list at once and because of the way it reconstructs the arguments list (adds a simple trailing "--" argument), it does not support arguments with spaces. (The GNU -Linux version of *getopt* provides flags that cause it to output a string quoted for a shell to work around this limitation, but this is not portable). This is a limitation in options handling in C Shells.

100: Rewrite the next script, using a more readable and clear logic.

```csh
#!/bin/csh

@ num = 0
echo "Enter a number between 0 and 223"
set num $<
if ( $num > 0 && $num <= 223 )
then
   if ( $num < 127 )
   then
      echo "Number may be first octet for class-A network IP"
   else
      if ( $num > 127 && $num <= 191 )
      then
         echo "Number may be first octet for class-B network IP"
      else
         if ( $num == 127 )
         then
            echo "Number is used for loopback"
         else
            echo "Number may be first octet for class-C network IP"
         endif
      endif
   endif
else
   echo "number is not usable for first octet in an IP address"
endif
```

Answer:

```
#!/bin/csh
@ num = 0
echo "Enter a number between 0 and 223"
set num $<
if ( $num <= 0 || $num > 223 )
then
    echo "number is not usable for first octet in an IP address"
    exit
endif

if ( $num == 127 )
then
    echo "Number is used for loopback"
    exit
endif

if ( $num < 127 )
then
    echo "Number may be first octet for class-A network IP"
    exit
endif

if ($num <= 191)
then
    echo "Number may be first octet for class-B network IP"
else
    echo "Number may be first octet for class-C network IP"
endif
```

It is easier for someone to follow this solution, but the order is important for the four if statements in this case. Note also the exit command in the first three if statements.

Chapter 4

Bash – Beginner

101: What is shebang?

Answer:

The #! symbol used in the first line of shell script is called the shebang. It is followed by the interpreter file and then an optional argument to execute it. At the same time, any line starting with a # can be considered as a comment and hence ignored by the shell. So, it is completely up to the shell to decide whether or not to compile the shebang.

102: What are pipes?

Answer:

Pipes let you pass the result of one shell program as the input to another shell program. The | or pipe symbol is used to create a pipe. The first program is executed, and its result is used as the input to the second program.

103: What is exit status?

Answer:

The exit status is a positive number or zero returned by a shell script after its execution. If the Exit status is zero, it means that the script has been executed successfully. Any number other than zero would mean an error. For each type of error, a different number is returned.

104: What is a subshell? How do you create it?

Answer:

Smaller subsections within a shell script that's contained within parenthesis are called subshells. While the subshell can access the variables outside of it, it cannot change their values except inside the subshell.

For example, you have a variable *var1* in the main shell which was initially assigned the value 5. Within a subshell, it was assigned the value 8. Within the subshell, it will have the value 8, but once outside the subshell, it will have the value 5 only.

105: Consider the following message:

"bash: scriptfile: Execute permission denied."

How could you fix it (assuming that you are the owner of scriptfile)?

Answer:

The user does not have permission to execute on *scriptfile*. We could run the following command to grant execute permission for everybody:

chmod +x scriptfile

106: The case statement is useful for comparing the value of a variable against a list of possible matches. True or false?

Answer:

TRUE

107: You don't remember the correct option (switch) for sort command, in order to sort some entries in reverse order. What could you do?

Answer:

Open the "man" page for sort command, run the command:

man sort

and then search the keyword "reverse" (the search starts using the /).

108: The first line of a shell script is:

#!/bin/bash

How does the shell interpret this line?

Answer:

The exec system call which is invoked to start a script will check the first two bytes of the script for a special sequence, #!, which specifies the interpreter executable to be used for executing this script, on the same line .

109: You need to find all files under your /home directory that were not accessed during last 10 days. What could you do?

Answer:

Run the following command:

find /home -type f -atime +10

110: How could you check if there are running *sshd* processes on your system?

Answer:

We could check by running the command:

ps - ef | grep sshd

or

pgrep sshd

111: What happens when you run the following command?

mkdir -p /tmp/{my,your,his,her}dir/{contacts,files}

a) 6 new directories will be created under the /tmp
b) 8 new directories will be created under the /tmp directory
c) 2 new directories will be created under the /tmp directory
d) It will not create new directories and an error message will be displayed.

Answer:

Option b) is correct. 8 new directories will be created.

112: The next line is the beginning of a conditional statement in a bash script:

if [[$1 = $var1 || = $var2]]

This statement has at least an error. Identify and correct it.

Answer:

There is a syntax error in test condition. In the second expression, there is no left part. Also, it is better to use double quotes around the variable substitution's expressions used in test, to ensure that syntax errors will not arise in case a variable is null or undefined. The correct statement is:

if [["$1" = "$var1" || "$1" = "$var2"]]

113: A for loop requires an arguments list. This list can result from:

    a) command substitution: for *var* in $(command) ....

    b) variable substitution: for *var* in $*anothervar* ....

    c) arguments given in the command line: for *var* in $* ....

    d) a test condition: for *var* in [["$*var*" -eq 3]] ....

    e) all the above

Answer:

Options a), b) as well as c) will give the desired result.

114: Given the following nested loops, which command would you use in place of command-to-process-file for the shell to execute the last *cat* command, if the test condition is met?

while true

do

    while true

    do

    echo "Please enter a filename:-->\c"

    read ans

    if [[-f "$ans"]]

>   then
>
>   command-to-process-file
>
>   fi
>
>   done
>
> done
>
> cat $ans

Answer:

break 2

115: What would happen if the following command was in the .bash_profile of a user?

trap ' ' INT

Answer:

The user could not interrupt any command started from that shell. The trap command would trap the *INT* signal, changing the behavior of the shell to ignore that signal.

116: The value of a variable should be compared against 8 possible values (and/or patterns) and some commands, different for each possible value, should be run. What is the structure that you would prefer for these checks?

Answer:

case "$var" in

pattern_1) ....

;;

;;

pattern_8) ....

;;

Esac

117: What is the expected output from the following command? *echo {a .. z}*

Answer:

It echoes all alphabetic lowercase characters, that is,

a b c d e f g h j k l m n o p q r s t u v w x y z

118: How can you run a job in the background?

Answer:

We can run a job in the background by adding the "&" in the end of the command line, that is, *command&*

119: What is the action performed by the command *cd -*?

Answer:

The command changes the current working directory to the previous working directory. It is equivalent to *cd $OLDPWD*.

120: Which are the special meanings of character ~ for the bash shell?

Answer:

The special meanings of character ~ are:

a) The ~ is equivalent to $HOME, that is, to the home directory of the user

b) ~dbuser1 corresponds to the home directory of user *dbuser1*, if there is such a user; otherwise, it is treated as the literal string ~dbuser1

c) ~+ means the current working directory, so it is equivalent to $PWD

d) ~- means the previous working directory, so it is equivalent to $OLDPWD

e) =~ is a regular expression match

121: What is the difference between *variable5* and $*variable5*?

Answer:

variable5 is the name of a variable, and $*variable5* is a reference to the value of this variable.

122: What is defined with the command *variable=value*, a local or an environment variable?

Answer:

A local variable is defined with the given command.

123: How can you find the bash shell version that is installed on your system?

Answer:

We can find the bash shell version of our system using:

echo $BASH_VERSION

For more details, use the array *BASH_VERSINFO*.

124: What does the bash built-in variable EDITOR do?

Answer:

The bash built-in variable EDITOR invokes the default editor, usually *vi* or *emacs*.

125: What is the purpose of shell built-in variable PATH?

Answer:

To define a list of paths to executables, PATH will be used by shell to find those files by their relative names.

126: Is there any way to declare an integer variable in bash?

Answer:

Yes, we can declare an integer variable in bash using the typeset *-i* command (or the equivalent declare).

127: How would the shell interpret the command "*echo ??a*"?

Answer:

Before starting the execution of *echo*, the shell will replace the two *??*. For the shell, the *?* represents any one character in a filename. But the first dot in a filename cannot be substituted by any character and should be given literally. This command would output any files and subdirectories in current directory, which have a name comprising of three characters, except the ones starting with a dot.

This page is intentionally left blank

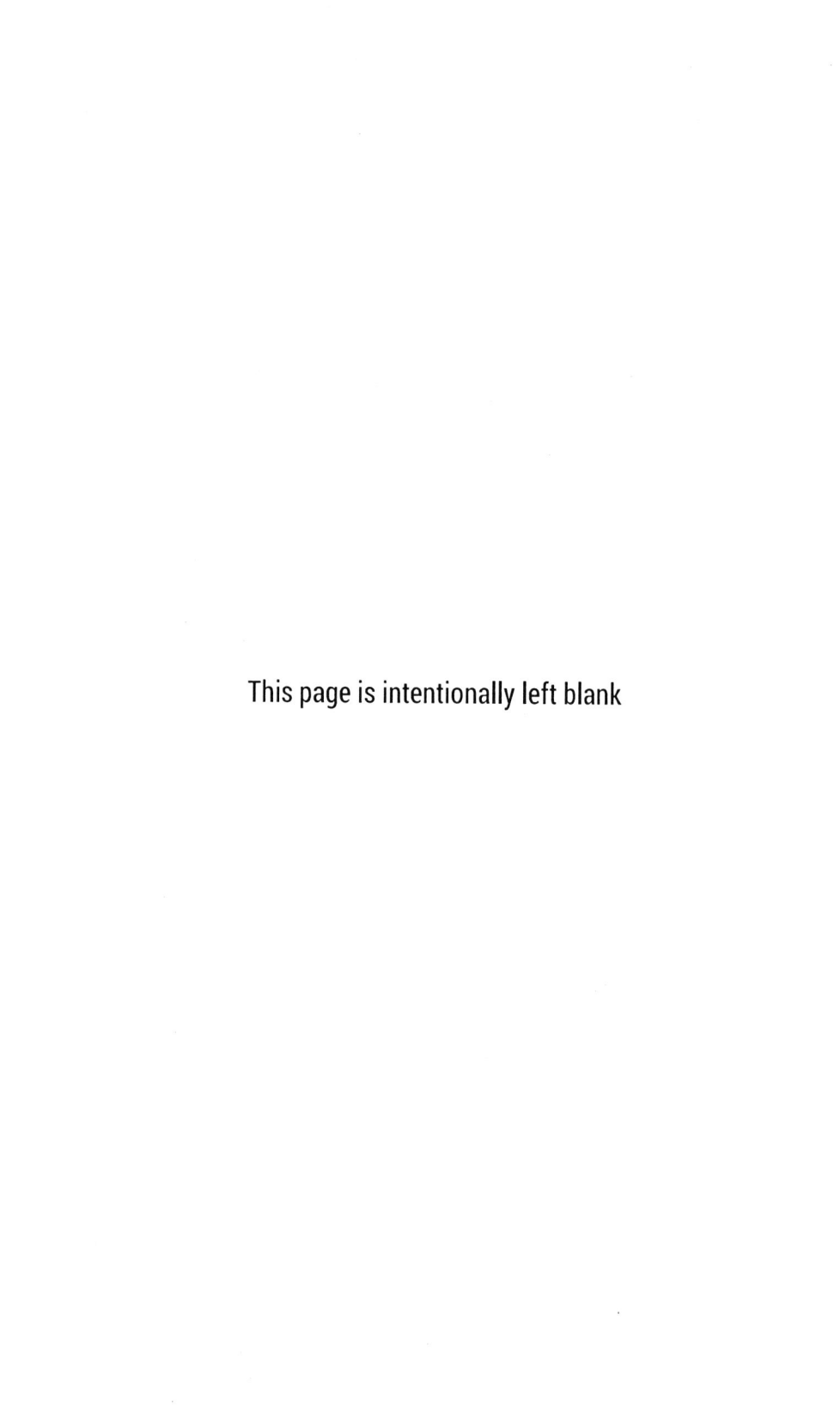

Chapter 5

Bash – Intermediate

128: Write a simple script that will check the numeric UID of the user executing it, will display a message and then will exit, if the user is not root.

Answer:

```
#!/bin/bash

if (( $(id -u) = 0 ))
then
    echo "Hello root"
else
    echo "You must login as root to execute this script!"
    exit 10
fi
exit
```

129: Construct a bash shell pattern to match any alphanumeric string ending with exactly one digit.

Answer:

*([a-zA-Z0-9])[a-za-Z][0-9]

130: Write a command that lists the filenames that match the pattern Name#_## exactly.

Answer:

The command to list the filenames that match the pattern Name#_## exactly is:

echo Name[0-9]_[0-9][0-9]

131: Write a command to get the list of all directory entries (files & subdirectories) that start with . (dot), except . (dot) and .. (double dot).

Answer:

The command is:

echo .[!.]*

132: You must check if a certain file exists on your system and if you have read access to it. Which syntax will you use?

Answer:

The syntax we would use is:

if [[-f filename && -r filename]]

then

echo "filename exists and it's readable"

else

echo "filename does not exist or is not readable"

Bash – Intermediate

fi

133: Consider the following snippet.

mail user << end

Hello,

Please check the last entries logged from that program in $(hostname):

$(tail -10 /var/opt/application/logfile)

EOF

end

What is the message to be sent to the user?

Answer:

The message to be sent to the user is:

Hello,

Please check the last entries logged from that program insystem's_hostname:

(the last 10 lines from the /var/opt/application/logfile)

EOF

134: What happens when you run this loop?

while read line

do

  echo $line

done <datafile

Answer:

The code reads the contents of datafile, line by line, and processes (here just displays) each line. It will finish when it reaches the end of file.

135: What happens when you run this loop?

while read line <datafile

do

   echo $line

done

Answer:

It is an infinite loop. Each iteration opens the datafile, reads only the first line, processes it (just displays it), and is repeated over and over.

136: You should find the entry that defines user account *dbuser1* from the *passwd* file.

grep 'dbuser1' /etc/passwd

Is the above command:
   a) correct,
   b) correct but not exact or sufficient, or
   c) completely insufficient,

Why?

Answer:

It is correct, but it is not exact or sufficient. This command will display all lines which contain the string *dbuser1* in any position, not only in the start of the line, and before the field separator (:).

The command which will return only the line starting with *dbuser1* will be as follows:

grep '^dbuser1:' /etc/passwd

137: Use the correct syntax to display all lines from the file named *datafile* that ends with the string *ing*. (a literal dot).

Answer:

grep 'ing\.$' datafile

138: A configuration file of an application (or service) contains many lines that are commented out, and just two or three useful lines. How could you display only the essential (uncommented) data?

Answer:

grep '^[^#]' conf_file

or

grep -v '^#' conf_file

139: How can the shell pass variables into *awk*?

Answer:

The shell passes variables into *awk* using the -v option of *awk* and the reserved word ENVIRON of the *awk* inside the *awk* statement.

e.g.:

var1="Some data"

awk -v Data="$var1" 'awk statement ...'

awk syntax using an existing exported variable:

ENVIRON["var"]

140: True or False: When input is provided to *awk*, *awk* will process every record.

Answer:

TRUE

141: True or False: All unquoted strings are treated as variables, keywords or functions in *awk* statements.

Answer:

TRUE

142: You have a simple (text) contacts file, containing lines in the following format:

name country

There is also a file for each country, each containing a different message.

How could you display the different file for each country, merged after each entry which contains that country?

Answer:

Create a file containing a sed function matching each country and inserting the corresponding file into the output. For example:

/USA/r usa_file

/Australia/r australia_file

then, use the following command:

sed -f functions_file contacts_file

143: True or False: In bash shell the array variables can be multi-dimensional.

Answer:

FALSE

Bash – Intermediate

144: How could you display the entire contents of an array variable?

Answer:

The entire contents of an array can be displayed by:

echo ${array[*]}

145: How could you get the length (the total number of elements) of an array?

Answer:

The length of an array can be found by:

echo ${#array[*]}

146: How could you initialize an array?

Answer:

An array can be initialized by:

set -A array value0 value1 ....

147: True or False: Array variables cannot be environment variables.

Answer:

TRUE

148: Is it possible to define a variable with local scope inside a function?

Answer:

Yes, it is possible to define a variable with local scope inside a function. If a variable is declared inside a function using the *declare* command or typeset, it exists only inside that function and is unset when function returns.

149: If you call a function using the syntax:

functionname /*

what will be the function's arguments (if any)?

Answer:

All the files & subdirectories under /, except dot files.

150: Is there any way to avoid overwriting the file when the following redirection syntax is used?

command > filename

Answer:

The shell option *noclobber* can be set to avoid overwriting the file.

151: Explain the following syntax:

command 2>&1 > /dev/null

Answer:

It redirects the *stderr* stream to file descriptor 1, that is, to the *stdout*, and then also redirects *stdout* to the special file */dev/null*, discarding both, output and errors.

152: What is the result of the command?

kill $$

Answer:

The given command kills (terminates) the current process.

153: Why is it preferable to use the TERM signal (-15) instead of the KILL signal (-9) in order to stop the execution of a process?

Answer:

The TERM signal "says" to the process to start its normal termination procedure, so it is a safe way to terminate processes, closing their open files and releasing the resources. The KILL signal just "shoots" the process, so that, if there were open file descriptors, they remain open.

154: Is it possible to change the default behavior of the shell when it receives a certain signal?

Answer:

Yes, it is possible to change the default behavior of the shell when it receives a certain signal using the *trap* command. But not all signals are 'trapable', e.g., the KILL signal is not a trapable signal.

155: What is the meaning of *$0* for an *awk* statement? What is the meaning of variables *$1, $2, ...* for the *awk*?

Answer:

awk reads each line of input as input record and splits each record in a set of numbered fields, in which the first field is *$1*, the second field is *$2*, and so on. The separator character used in this process is the value of *awk* special variable FS. The *$0* represents the entire record.

156: Is it possible to define some actions to be performed before the processing of the input lines by the *awk* command?

Answer:

Yes, it is possible by using the reserved word BEGIN and putting the actions inside a block {}.

157: Select all of the following that apply to bash shell variables. Explain all that do not apply.

a) Bash variables are untyped, by default
b) Although bash variables are basically treated as strings, the bash shell permits integer operations and comparisons on variables
c) All variables defined in a process (or shell) are local or private variables, that is, they are known only to that process
d) The variable names can contain any character, including special characters

Answer:

Options a) and b) apply to bash shell variables.

Option c) does not apply. If variables have not been exported, yes, they are of local scope, otherwise are "inherited" from any sub-process.

Option d) does not apply. The variables names can contain only alphanumerical characters and underscores, and the first character could not be a digit.

158: True or False: A script invoked from the command line can export variables back to its parent shell.

Answer:

FALSE

159: Write the echo command which will display the following line, using " (double quotes).

Some of Bash shell's special characters are: $, #, <, <<, >, >>, \, ', ", `, {,}

Answer:

echo "Some of Bash shell's special characters are: \$, #, <, <<, >, >>, \\, ', \", \`, \{, \}"

160: How could you define your primary prompt to reflect the login name, the "at" sign, the system's hostname and the current working directory?

Answer:

$PS1="\u@\h \w >"$

161: How can you set the value of a variable to the contents of a file?

Answer:

We can set the value of a variable to the contents of a file using:

a) *variable =`cat file1`* (using command substitution with *cat*, thus with slower execution than the next one)

b) *variable=`<file1`* (using command substitution with redirection)

162: What are the differences between the two forms of command substitution, $(cmd) and `cmd`?

Answer:

The differences between the two forms of command substitution are:

a) The newer form $(cmd) permits nesting, e.g.,

  count=$(wc -w $(ls -l | awk '{print $9}'))

b) The two forms treat differently the double backslashes:

  echo `echo \\` will display an empty line, but

echo $(echo \ \) will display one \.

163: Describe the "and" list execution.

Answer:

An "and" list is a way of chaining together commands. The syntax is:

command 1 && command 2 && ... command-n

Each command is executed in turn, provided the previous one has given an exit value of TRUE. At the first FALSE return value, the chain terminates, and the remaining commands do not get executed.

164: Bash shell (version 4.2) permits representing and displaying characters in foreign alphabets. How? Give an example displaying the mathematical symbol PI.

Answer:

Bash supports the Unicode escape \u and \U. The command:

echo -e '\u220F'

displays the PI (π).

165: Give the output of the following code snippet.

a=5

let "val = a<6?1:2"

echo $val

let a++

let "val = a<6?2:3"

echo $val

Answer:

1 (from the first echo)

3 (from the second echo)

166: The permissions on a directory /mydir are rw-r---- and you are the owner of this directory. Can you display the contents of /mydir? Can you change directory to /mydir? Can you create a new file under /mydir? Can you read the contents of a file contained in /mydir?

Answer:

Without the execute permission, you can change your current working directory to that directory, but you cannot use a trailing / (like in /mydir/) in any way. So, you can only execute the *ls* command to display the contents of this directory, but not *ls -l*, so it is not possible to get a long listing of this directory. You cannot execute a command like *cat /mydir/file1*, so it's impossible to access any file under the /mydir, regardless of its permissions, and it is also not possible to create a file there, since the syntax /mydir/ is not permitted.

167: Which are the two valid syntax forms to declare a function?

Answer:

a) *function function_name {*
   commands
   }

b) *function_name() {*
   commands
   }

168: Correct the following function's declaration.

holder() { echo "Press Return to continue...." ; read dummy }

Answer:

holder() { echo "Press Return to continue...." ; read dummy ; } # missing semicolon before }

169: What does the += operator perform?

Answer:

In a numerical context, integer arithmetic (*let var+=1*)

In a string context, string concatenation (*string+=value*)

Chapter 6

Bash – Advanced

170: Explain *whiptail*, *man* and *grep*.

Answer:

A *whiptail* in shell script lets you show user-friendly dialogue boxes to display information or to take user input.

The *man* command is like the help and info commands used to seek help. The difference is that *man* displays the *roffhelp* (*roff* being the first UNIX program with text formatting).

The *grep* is a utility that's used to search for information in pipes or files. It is used for text search along with other commands, such as the *ls* command. Suppose you are looking for a file with *mynm* in its name, you can redirect the output of *ls* command to a *grep* command with the text to search for and you will get the file which has it.

171: Explain /dev and /proc.

Answer:

The /dev folder contains the files with hardware information. The device files are stored in this folder. It may have information on devices that may not be available in the hardware also. You can also load external file systems as if it were a single file.

The /proc folder is a mirror that contains information on the processes, utilities and programs that are currently running in the system.

172: Explain *trap* command.

Answer:

The *trap* is used for debugging the signals or errors sent by the system when a program runs. The *trap* receives the signal sent by the system which is then processed in the script. It is like exception handling in C++ or Java.

173: What is POSIX?

Answer:

The POSIX character set lets you specify a range of characters without using the wildcards. They are more readable and easier to use than the wildcards. Moreover, POSIX lets you capture the control characters and graphics which is not possible with wildcards. For example, [:alpha:] denotes all alphabets from A-Z and a-z.

174: Explain *tput* and *infocmp*.

Answer:

The *tput* command lets you initialize the terminal or access the

Bash – Advanced

information in it. You can use the *tput* command with many options to control various terminal functions. For example, *tput clear* lets you clear the screen, *tput reset* will reset the parameters set in the terminal and clear the screen.

The *infocmp* command is used to get in-depth details about the current terminal. It takes information from the *terminfo* database.

175: What kind of problems would occur if you define a function named *ls*?

Answer:

The function preempts or overrides the *ls* command if we define a function named *ls*.

176: Define a function named *pause_until_return*, to pause the execution of the script until the user presses the return key.

Answer:

function pause_until_return () {

echo "Press RETURN to continue ...."

read dummy

}

177: How can you create a functions library and what are the advantages of such a library?

Answer:

You can create a functions "library" file, that is, a file that contains functions declarations and common variables definitions, and then 'source' that "library file" from any script that needs to call any of these functions:

#!/bin/bash

. /path_to_library/library_file #mind the dot (.)

The advantages of using the function libraries are:

a) It reduces the size of shell script files
b) Updates are easily available. If a function library file is used by many scripts and the contents of the function file are modified, the updated version is immediately available to all scripts that call that function

178: Is it permissible to use recursive functions (functions that call themselves)?

Answer:

Yes, it is permissible to use recursive functions. But we must be careful not to start a kind of "infinite loop".

179: The following code snippet uses a file descriptor in order to create a file:

exec 3> /tmp/newfile

echo -u3 "First line ...."

echot -u3 "Second line ..."

exec 3>&-

The following code snippet creates the same exact file:

echo "First line ..." > /tmp/newfile

echo "Second line ...." >> /tmp/newfile

But there is an important difference in the way of functioning of the above snippets. Could you explain it?

Answer:

The first snippet opens the *newfile* once, with the *exec 3>*, and then the file remains open until the execution of the second exec.

In the second snippet, the file is opened first time during the first *echo* command, then closes, then is opened again when the second *echo* starts, and then is closed again. This could be an important issue from performance's perspective, if this syntax will be used many times (e.g., inside a loop)

180: If you should use an interactive command (like *sftp*) in a script, what could you use in order to automate this function (without user interaction)?

Answer:

We could use the so called "here" document.

181: What is the output of the following?

netstat -rn | awk '/^def/ {print "Default gateway is ", $2}'

Answer:

The string "Default gateway is " followed by the IP Address of the defined default gateway.

182: What is the output of the following command?

*awk -F: '{BEGIN {OFS="=="} ; $2 = "****"; print NR "\t" $0}' /etc/passwd*

Answer:

The numbered lines of */etc/passwd*, where the password field has been replaced by the string "****" and the separator ":" by the "==".

183: Explain the following pipeline.

grep bash file1 | diff file2 -

Answer:

The hyphen (-) is used to pipe *stdout* from the second command to other commands. Here, the pipeline compares the lines which contain the string "*bash*" from file1, to the entire contents of file2.

184: How could you declare an associative array?

Answer:

declare -A assoc

185: Which syntax returns (expands to) the indexes in an array ARRAY?

Answer:

${!ARRAY[@]}

or

${!ARRAY[*]}

186: What is the built-in *mapfile* command used for?

Answer:

The built-in *mapfile* command is used to assign lines of standard input (and from a file with redirection) to an array defined by an argument, each line in a separate element. If no array is given in the command line, the default array name is MAPFILE. The target array must be an integer indexed array (not an associative one).

187: Write an equivalent but shorter form of the following if structure, without using if.

if [[$# -eq 0]]

then

    dirpath=$(pwd)

else

   dirpath=$@

fi

Answer:

[[$# -eq 0]] && dirpath=$(pwd) || dirpath=$@

188: Give the output of the following snippet and explain it.

a='$val1'

val1='$val2'

val2=newval

echo $a

eval echo $a

eval eval echo $a

Answer:

a) *$val1* (first echo: single quotes do not permit any substitution)

b) *$val2* (second echo - *eval*: the invocation of *eval* forces a reevaluation of its arguments, so the *arg $a* is replaced by the value of *a*, that is, *$val1*; then *$val1* is replaced by the value of *val1*, that is, *$val2*)

c) *newval* (last line: The second invocation of *eval* causes another re-evaluation of its argument, which is *$val2*, thus, replacing it with the value of *val2*, *newval*.)

189: Set the positional parameters to a string then unset the positional parameters and then set them again to their original values.

Answer:

new_positionals="Another string to be assigned to the positional parameters word by word"

orig_args=$@

echo $@ # Displays the current positionals params

set -- $new_positionals

echo $@ # Displays the contents of new_positionals

set --

echo $@ # Displays an empty line

set -- $orig_args

echo $@ # Displays the original args

190: The rm command just unlinks the file (*inode*) from the data blocks. To properly delete a file, it is required to overwrite the blocks occupied by the file. Create a script to securely delete the files passed to it as arguments.

Answer:

for i

do

dd if=/dev/null of="$i" bs=1024 count=`expt 1 + `stat "$i" | grep 'Size:' | awk '{print $2}'` / 1024`

done

191: Assuming there is a defined array named Array, what does this for loop do?

for i in ${!Array[@]}

do

   echo ${Array[i]}

done

Bash – Advanced

Answer:

It displays all the elements in Array. The notation ${!array[@]} expands to all the indices of the array.

192: What is the impact of using the terminator characters ;;& and ;& in a case structure?

Answer:

The ;;& terminator continues to the next pattern test. The ;& terminator executes the next statement even with a dummy pattern, that is, it executes the next statement even if the value does not match the pattern, so it is somewhat less useful and should be used with care.

193: Write the output of the following case, assuming that
  a) $1 equals to a, and
  b) $1 equals to 5:

case "$1" in

  [[:print:]])echo "$1 is a printable character.";;&

  [[:alnum:]]) echo "$1 is an alpha/numeric character.";;&

  [[:alpha:]]) echo "$1 is an alphabetic character.";;&

  [[:lower:]]) echo "$1 is a lowercase alphabetic character.";;&

  [[:digit:]]) echo "$1 is an numeric character.";&

  @@%%)echo "Dummy";;*

esac

Answer:

  a) a is a printable character
     a is an alpha/numeric character
     a is an alphabetic character

a is a lowercase alphabetic character
b) 5 is a printable character
5 is an alpha/numeric character
5 is a numeric character
Dummy

194: Name two ways to set an array to the contents of a text file.

Answer:

a) *declare -a ARRAY*

 # Link filedescriptor 10 with stdin

exec 10<&0

exec < logfile

let count=0

while read LINE

do

ARRAY[$count]=$LINE

((count++))

done

b) *ARRAY=(`cat logfile `)*

195: Name a limitation of *getopts* bash built-in.

Answer:

There are a couple of restrictions while using the *getopts* bash built-in:

a) No support for lengthy names with ## prefix
b) Support only for shorter one-character options

Bash – Advanced

196: Debug the following script excerpt.

number=1

while ["$number" <5]
do
  echo -n "$number "
  let "number += 1"
done

Answer:
It should be:
number=1
while ["$number" -lt 5]
do
  echo -n "$number "
  let "number += 1"
done

197: Debug the following script excerpt.

function add_args ()
{
  echo "Adding two numbers"
  let "sumval = $1 + $2"
  echo $sumval
}

num1=42
num2=11
echo "Sum of $num1 and $num2 = $(add2 $num1 $num2)"

Answer:

function add_args ()
{
 # echo "Adding two numbers"
 # The output of this function is captured, and the two echo
 # commands concatenate.
   let "sumval = $1 + $2"
   echo $sumval
}

num1=42
num2=11
echo "Sum of $num1 and $num2 = $(add2 $num1 $num2)"

198: Write a script that replaces every occurrence of a pattern with another in a given file. The script receives 3 arguments: *pattern_to_be_replaced substitution_pattern filename*

Answer:

#!/bin/bash
if [$# -ne 3]
then
   echo "Usage: `basename $0` old-pattern new-pattern filename"
   exit 70
fi

old_p=$1
subst_p=$2

if [-f "$3"]

Bash – Advanced

```
then
    filename=$3
else
    echo "File \"$3\" does not exist."
    exit 70
fi
sed -e "s/$old_p/$subst_p/g" $filename
```

199: Create a function that capitalizes the first character of its string arguments.

Answer:

```
capital_char ()
{
    org_string="$@"
    for str in $@
    do
        firstchar=${str:0:1}
        rest_string=${str:1}
        FirstChar=`echo "$firstchar" | tr a-z A-Z`
        cap_string=${cap_string}" "$FirstChar$rest_string")
    done
}
```

200: What does the following code snippet do?

```
declare -A files
find . -type f -exec sha1sum {} + | while read -r sum fname
do
```

```
if [[ ${files[$sum]} ]]
then
    printf 'rm -- "%s" '
else
    files[$sum]="$fname"
fi
done> duplics
```

Answer:

It checks for duplicate files using a hash table (associative array) indexed with the SHA sum of the files in the current directory. *sha1 sum* computes and checks SHA1 message digest. It prints or checks SHA1 (160-bit) checksums. This list passes through the while read loop to variables *sum* and *fname*. Then the script checks if there is already an element associated with the index $sum in the array files. If so, it is a duplicate file, and displays an "*rm*" message. Otherwise, the filename is added to the array files as a new element associated with the index $sum.

201: Describe the functionality of the following script.

```
#!/bin/bash

RESULT=mycgi.pl
(
cat <<'EOF'
#!/bin/perl
foreach $dir (split /:/, $ENV{PATH} ) {
    echo "$dir\n";
}
```

Bash – Advanced   97

EOF

) > $RESULT

Answer:

This script creates a *perl* script named *mycgi.pl*. The whole *perl* script is contained in "here" document. The end mark of "here" document (*EOF*) is enclosed in backquotes, thus disabling parameter substitution, so all lines in "here" document are treated and output as literal text.

202: Explain the following code snippet.

t=traffic

traffic=intolerable

echo "\"traffic\" = $traffic"

echo -n "dereferenced \"t\" = "

eval echo \$$t

t=traffic

traffic=unbelievable

unbelievable=intolerable

echo "Changing value of \"traffic\" to $traffic."

echo "\"traffic\" now is $traffic"

echo -n "dereferenced \"t\" now is"

eval echo \$$t

Answer:

The use of *\$$variable* in conjunction with *eval* means indirect reference - *dereference*. First $ is escaped and pasted on to the value of var. Variable *t* holds the name of another variable, and in second block, this variable (traffic) holds the value of another variable. The output produced by this snippet is:

"traffic"=intolerable

dereferenced "t"=intolerable

Changing value of "traffic" to unbelievable.

"traffic" now is unbelievable

dereferenced "t" now is intolerable

203: Which is the modern indirect reference form that is equivalent to the old one (*eval var1=\$$var2*)?

Answer:

${!variable}

eval var1=\$$var2   <=>   var1=${!var2}

204: Explain this code snippet.

coproc { cat datafile; sleep 2; }

while read -u ${COPROC[0]} record

do

  echo "$record" | cut -c2-

done

kill $COPROC_PID

Answer:

The *coproc* builtin enables two parallel processes to communicate and interact. This co-process communicates with the while read loop. ${*COPROC*[0]} is the file descriptor of the co-process. So, the while-read loop reads file *datafile* line by line and removes the first character of each line from the output. At the end, when there is no longer need of the co-process, it kills its PID ($*COPROC_PID*).

205: The following excerpt does not achieve to set the 3 variables (my_var1, my_var2, my_var3). Explain.

my_var1=31

my_var2=7

my_var3=17

coproc echo " three1 sevenoneseven"

while read -u ${COPROC[0]} my_var1 my_var2 my_var3;

do

  echo "Inside my while-read loop1: ";

  echo "p = $p"; echo "q = $q"; echo "r = $r"

  echo "coprocmy_file descriptor: ${COPROC[0]}"

done

echo "Outside my_ while-read loop1: ";

echo "p = $p"; echo "q = $q"; echo "r = $r"

echo "coprocmy_file descriptor1: ${COPROC[0]}"

Answer:

Inside the loop, everything is fine. The output will be:

Inside my_while-read loop1:

p = three

q = seven

r = oneseven

coprocmy_ file descriptor1:#some descriptor

Since this loop runs in a subshell, the values do not sustain. Hence, the output of the three echo commands will be:

p=

q=

r=

The coprocess is still running, but the values are lost.

206: Write a script that recognizes and handles only the command options -l (followed by a value) and -m in any order. An invalid option will cause the script to terminate with an error, displaying the invalid option.

Answer:

#!/bin/bash

 # Usage: script [-l -m]

while getopts :l:m flag

do

   case $flag in

   l) echo "Option has $OPTAGR as its value" ;;

   m) echo "Option -m received";;

   *)echo "Invalid option $OPTARG";;

done

207: Give an example of downloading a URL using Bash shell.

Answer:

exec 3<>/dev1/my_tcp/www.abcnet.cn1/80

echo -e "GET1 / HTTP/1.0\n" >&3

cat<&3

When a command is executed on the file /dev1/my_tcp_2/$host1/$port_ pseudo-device2, TCP connection will be opened by 'Bash' to the associated socket. Hence it may issue a HTTP GET.

208: Write the code to return a randomly selected index of an array (integer indexed), selecting a random element of the array.

Answer:

Array=(`ls -a`) # Initialize an array

R_INDEX=$(($RANDOM%${#Array[@]})) #${Array[@]} returns the length of Array

$RANDOM%${#Array[@]} returns random integer between 1 and length of array

R-ELEM=${Array[$R_INDEX]}

echo "Randomly selected element is $R_ELEM with index number $R_INDEX"

209: Write a snippet to return a randomly selected string index of an associative array and the element associated with this index.

Answer:

declare -A ass_array

ass_array[John]="john.k@domain1.com"

ass_array[Chris]="chris.sm@hotmail.com"

ass_array[Angela]="angela.st@domain5.com"

indices=(${!ass_array[*]})

count=${#indices[@]}

r_index_pos=$(($RANDOM%${#indices[@]}))

r_index=${indices[$r_index_pos]}

r_element=${ass_array[$r_index]}

echo "Randomly selected element is $r_element with index $r_index"

210: Name the obvious advantage of an "and" list.

Answer:

The obvious advantage of an "and" list is that they can effectively replace complex if/then and/or case structures.

Chapter 7

Basics

211: What are the types of files used in UNIX?

Answer:

The types of files used in UNIX are:
   a) **Ordinary File:** Contains text, instructions and data
   b) **Special File:** Allows to access a file using its alias or shortcut
   c) **Directory:** Contains both ordinary and special files

212: Which type of file's name starts with '.'?

Answer:

Name of the hidden file usually starts with '.' and contains the configuration information. These files will not be shown while using *ls* command.

213: How will you display the file name starting with the particular letters say 'hel'?

Answer:

We can display the file name starting with particular letters using '*'. It is a meta-character used with *ls* to display the specified files.

Example:

ls hel.txt*

-Displays the file names starting with 'hel' and ending with 'txt'

214: Which characters are called meta-characters?

Answer:

The following characters are called meta-characters:

a) '*' and '?'

b) '*' display the files -starting with the specified characters

c) '?' display the file names that match with the given single character

215: How does the interaction between user and UNIX system take place?

Answer:

The interaction between user and UNIX system takes place as follows:

a) Using 'shell' interface

b) Gets the input from the user, executes the function and returns the result

c) Based on the operating system, shell types also vary

216: What is the purpose of '$'?

Answer:

'$' is called command prompt and it allows the user to enter the command. It determines the command from the first word of the input.

Example:

$> cal -5

217: What is the purpose of '#'?

Answer:

'#' is used to comment the lines. When used in the first line followed by '!', it denotes the location of the shell.

Example:

#!/ki/*my_shell1*/firstscript1

218: How will you know the functionality of a command in UNIX?

Answer:

The functionality of a command in UNIX can be known using *man* command. It gives the name, description and parameters required for the command.

Example: $*man date*

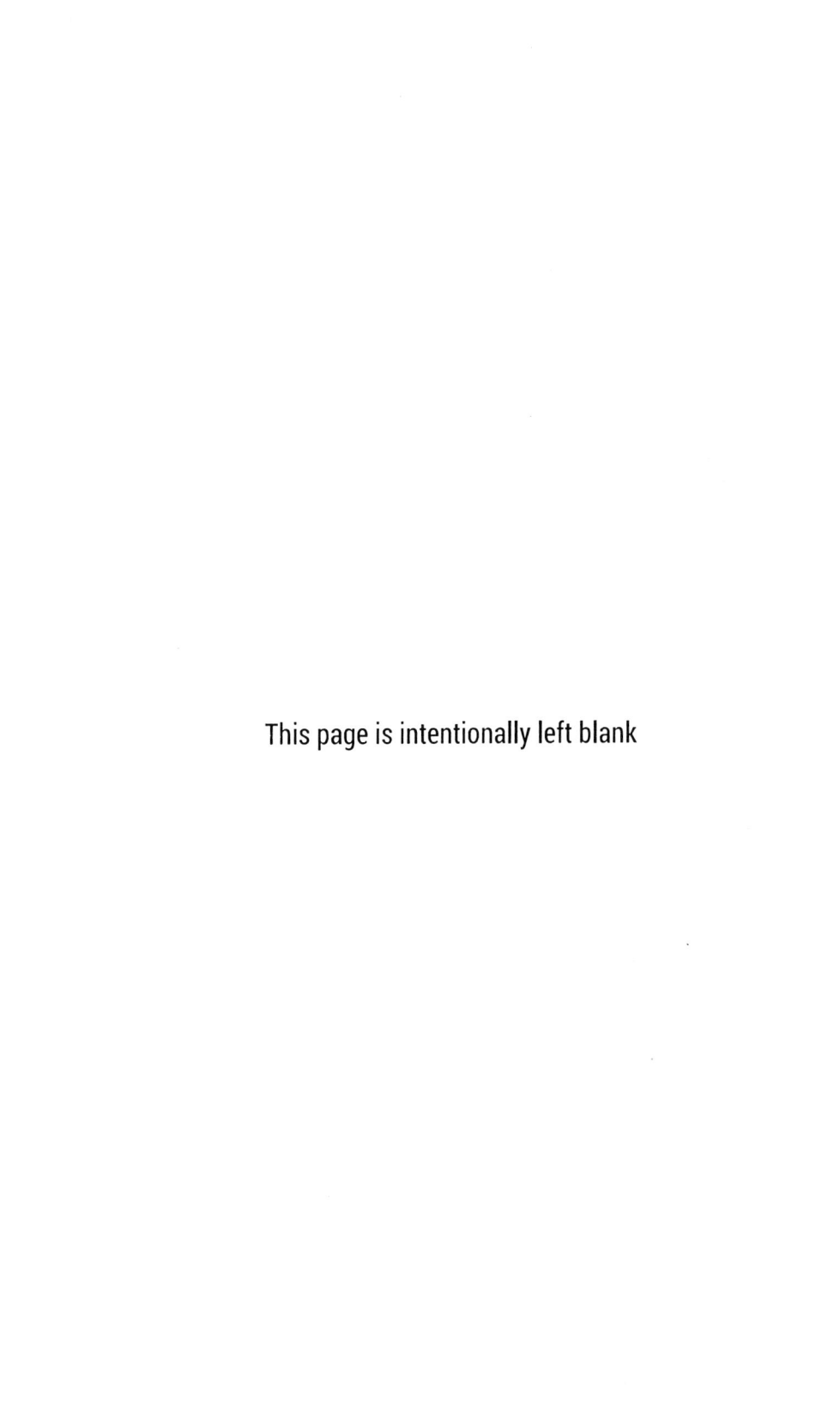

Chapter 8

Commands

219: Explain the commands *getty* and *agetty*.

Answer:

The *getty* command is a short form for "get*tty*" to manage the virtual terminals or teletypes in UNIX. Though TTY was meant for teletypes, it is not used to connect to all types of virtual machines. In Linux, the *agetty* command is used instead of *getty*.

220: Explain *strace* and *ltrace*.

Answer:

The *strace* command lets you trace all the system calls or signals. This helps to debug the programs. The *ltrace* lets you trace the library calls for debugging the program. The *strace* call is made by the program to trace the kernel. The *ltrace* is called by the program to trace the library.

221: Explain the commands *nice* and *pidof*.

Answer:

The *nice* command changes the priority of a background job. Its variations are *renice* that resets the priority of a running process and *snice* that resets the priority of multiple processes. The *pidof* command is used to know the identity of a running job process. It is essentially the Process ID of a particular job. It is usually used to kill that process.

222: Explain *lockfile*.

Answer:

A *lockfile* is a file that controls the permissions to a device, file or a resource. It is a utility that lets you create the file that contains the permissions or locks set for another file or device. Usually, the locks are checked in the /var/lock directory. However, when the *lockfile* is used, the locks and permissions are checked in it instead. The *lockfile* is also used to block the browsers from accessing your mail folders.

223: Explain *env*.

Answer:

The *env* command is used to change a few environment variables only for running a particular script without changing the system environment. You can set the *env* in the shebang line. For example, you can set the scripting language to Perl for a particular script only using *env* instead of changing the environment settings.

224: Which command is used to list the hidden files in a directory?

Answer:

a) *ls*: list all the files in the directory

b) *ls -a*: list the hidden files in the directory

225: How will you redirect the output to a file?

Answer:

We can redirect the output to a file using '>'.

For example,

ls> myfile1

'ls' displays the files and '>' redirects these contents to the file names '*myfile1*'

226: How will you search for a pattern in a file?

Answer:

We can search for a pattern in a file using *grep* command.

Example:

grep my_pattern1 myfilename1

-search my_pattern1 in the file '*myfilename1*'

227: How will you append the output of a command to a file?

Answer:

We can append the output of a command to a file using '>>' symbol.

Example:

ls>> myfile2

-Output of the 'ls' command will be appended to the 'myfile2'

228: What is the purpose of '2>' in UNIX shell?

Answer:

It redirects the error of a program to a specified file.

Example:

myprogram 2> myfileerr2

-Redirects the error of the *'myprogram2'* to the file *'myfileerr2'*

229: How will you get the output of a previous command as an input to the subsequent command?

Answer:

We can get the output of a previous command as an input to the subsequent command using *'pipeline(|)'*.

Example:

ls –s | grep mysearch1

'ls' gives the list of file names and the names that match with the *'mysearch1'* will be output to the user.

230: Which commands are used to print the nth line of a file?

Answer:

sed or *head* commands are used to print the nth line of a file.

Syntax:

Sed –n '<line number> p' my_file.txt

head –<n> my_file1.txt | tail -1

Example:

To print the *7th* line of the file,

sed –n '7 p' my_file1.txt

head –7 my_file1.txt | tail -1

231: How will you search for a file in folders?
Answer:

We can search for a file in folders using *grep* command.

Example:

grepki my_folder1/folder2

ki - file name

folder1 and *folder2* - file's path

To ignore cases, use *'i'*

grep -i "ki" my_folder1/folder2

232: What is the purpose of '-r' and '-v' in *grep* command?
Answer:

The purpose of *'-r'* and *'-v'* in *grep* command are:

a) It searches recursively for the pattern in all files

   Example:

   grep –r "name" /myfold1/myfile1

b) *'-v'* – display the lines that does not contain the given word

   Example:

   grep –v "name" /myfold1/myfile1

233: How will find a directory of a file?
Answer:

We can find the directory of a file using *'ff'*. It returns the directory in which the file is present. The starting letter of the file name can also be given.

Example:

ff myfile2

234: How will you kill a process?

Answer:

We can kill a process using *kill* command. Id of the process should be known to kill a process. It can be retrieved by using *ps* command.

Example:

kill 22230

235: What are the ways to create a file?

Answer:

A file can be created in the following ways:

  a) Using *vi* command. The files can be edited using *cat* command

   Example:

   vi my_filename2

  b) Using *emacs*. It is a type of editor that allows to create and edit a file

   Example:

   emacs my_filename2

236: What are the ways to get name of the 'cpu' model?

Answer:

The ways to get the name of the *'cpu'* model are:

Commands

a) Using *'grep'*. "*grep –i 'model' /proc/mycpuinfo*" returns the model name
b) Using *grep* with pipeline command. "*#cat /proc/mycpuinfo | grep –i 'model'* "returns the model name of 'cpu'

237: How will you get the number of words in a file?
Answer:

We can get the number of words in a file using *wc* command. It returns total number of lines, words, bytes and name of the file.

Example:

wc myfile_name1

This page is intentionally left blank

Chapter 9

Variables and Arrays

238: What are positional parameters?

Answer:

Positional parameters are the arguments passed to a script from the command prompt. It is usually denoted by the number of its position such as $0, $1, $2 etc. After $9, the positional parameters are accessed with ${10}, ${11} etc. with the position within braces. $* and $@ denotes all the parameters.

239: Explain the *shift* command.

Answer:

The *shift* command will shift the positional parameters one position to its left. So, with the *shift* command, $3 will be $2 and $2 will be $1 and so on and so forth. For all positions in two digits or more, you have to use them within braces.

240: Does = and -*eq* function similarly?

Answer:

The = is usually used as the assignment operator, that is, to assign values to a variable. The == is used for comparison. The -*eq* command is also used for comparison. The difference is that while == does a lexical or string comparison, -*eq* does a numeric comparison.

241: How will you initialize and print the values in UNIX?

Answer:

Initialization:

my_variable="my_value" //without any space before or after equal sign

Print:

echo $my_variable

242: How will you concatenate the variables in UNIX?

Answer:

We can concatenate the variables in UNIX using '$'.

Example:

my_var1="Good"

my_var2="$my_var1 Morning"

my_var3="$my_var2 Ki"

echo $my_var3 //Good Morning Ki

243: How will you make a variable read-only?

Answer:

We can make a variable read-only by using *readonly*. After

Variables and Arrays

setting the variable to read only mode, changing the variable generates error.

Example:

my_var1="Status"

readonly my_var1

my_var1="Cool" //error

244: How will you delete a variable?

Answer:

We can delete a variable using *unset*. The variables that are 'read-only' cannot be deleted.

Example:

my_var1="Status"

unset my_var1

echo $ my_var1 //nothing will be printed

245: What are the types of variables?

Answer:

The different types of variables are:

a) **Environment:** Accessed by child processes of the shell

b) **Local:** Accessed by present instance of the shell

c) **Shell:** set and used by shell

246: How will you get the file name and number of arguments accepted by the current script?

Answer:

We can get the file name and the number of arguments accepted by the current script using '$0' and '$#' with *echo* command.

a) **$0**: returns the file name
b) **$#**: returns the number of arguments accepted by the script

247: How will you get the status of the last executed command?
Answer:

We can get the status of the last executed command using '$?'. It returns a numerical value. It returns '0' for successful execution, '1' for unsuccessful execution and other values representing some kind of errors.

248: How will you achieve 'do-while' looping?
Answer:

#!/bin/sh

my_cnt1=$9#Initialization

while [$my_cnt1 -gt 5]#condition

do

echo $my_cnt1Hellllo!

my_cnt1=$(expr $my_cnt -1) #decrement

done

echo COMPLETED!!

249: How will you call a function in UNIX?
Answer:

Syntax:

my_var1=$(function_name1 $my_arg1 $my_arg2)

Variables and Arrays

function_name - function to be called

my_arg1,my_arg2 - arguments to be passed

250: What are the ways to get the process id of a shell?

Answer:

The different ways to get the process id of a shell are:

a) Using *'ps'*. It lists all the processes with the corresponding details like id, name, etc

Example:

ps –u my_name3

b) Using *'$$'*. It returns the process id of the current shell

Example:

echo $$

251: How will you initialize an array?

Answer:

my_arrvar1 [index]=my_val

Example:

status1[0]= "Good"

status1[1]= "Excellent"

a) In 'ksh' shell, initialization will be

set –A my_arrvar1 my_val1 my_val2 …my_valn

b) In 'bash' shell

my_arrvar1=(my_val1 my_val2 … my_valn)

252: How will you access the array variables?

Answer:

a) Using '$'

www.vibrantpublishers.com

Example:

echo ${my_arrvar1[1]}

To access all the values of an array:

a) Use '[*]'

Example:

echo ${my_arrvar1[@]}

b) Use '[@]'

Example:

echo ${my_arrvar1[@]}

Chapter 10

Special Shell Variables

253: Explain the special shell variables.

Answer:

Shell has some special variables which offer special values that are otherwise not accessible within the script or program. Here are some of the special shell variables commonly used:

a) $0: current script's filename

b) $#: the number of arguments passed on while calling a script

c) #?: The exit status of the script

d) $$: gives out the process id of the script

254: How do you check if a string is empty with an operator?

Answer:

Checking an empty string is not possible with the usual comparison operators. You cannot use == to check if the string is empty. The -eq command also cannot be used for string comparison. Instead, the -z operator is used to check for empty string. To check if the string is not empty, the -n operator can be used.

255: Describe the purpose of 'killring('')'.

Answer:

a) It indicates how many killed strings will be in memory. Default value is '30'

b) It keeps only most recently killed memory when set less than '2' or 'unset'

256: Describe the purpose of 'matchbeep('')'.

Answer:

a) When set to 'never', it never beeps on completion

b) When set to 'nomatch', it beeps when no match is found

c) When set to 'ambiguous', it beeps on multiple matches

257: How will you list jobs?

Answer:

a) Using 'listjobs('')'. When a job is suspended, list all the jobs

b) When set to 'long', listing will be in 'long' format

258: Describe the purpose of 'correct('')'.

Answer:

a) When set to 'cmd', it provides automatic spelling correction of commands

b) When set to 'complete', it provides automatic completion of

Special Shell Variables

commands

c) When set to 'all', it provides automatic correction for entire line

259: What are the functions of *echo_style()*?

Answer:

a) When set to 'bsd', if the first argument is '-n', new line will not be displayed

b) When set to 'sysv', it interprets backslash as escape sequence characters

c) When set to 'bsd', it accepts both '-n' and escape sequence

260: How will you set the mode of the editor?

Answer:

We can set the mode of the editor using *inputmode('')*. When set to "overwrite" or "insert" mode at the beginning of each line, it sets the editor to that mode.

261: How will you avoid duplicate entries in the memory?

Answer:

We can avoid duplicate entries in the memory using *killdup('')*. When set to 'all', only unique string will be entered into the kill ring. When set to 'prev', the entry that is same as the one that is already in ring will not be allowed to enter into the kill ring.

This page is intentionally left blank

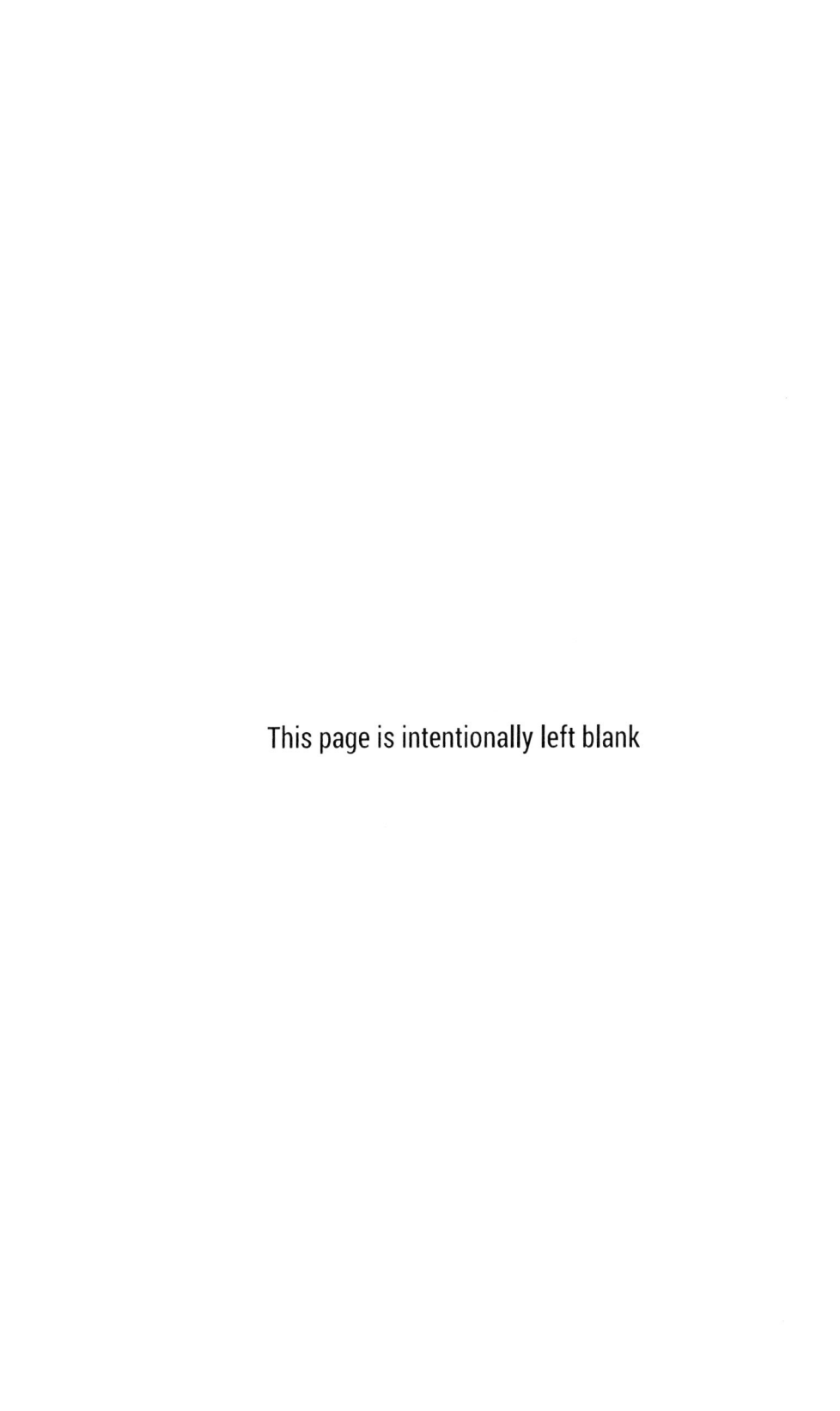

Chapter 11

Operators and Shell Substitutions

262: What are the different types of substitutions available in shell?

Answer:

When some special characters are used in the script, it is substituted by its value. For example, \n is substituted by a new line, \\ is substituted by \, \b is substituted by backspace. There are more substitutions available in shell. Command substitution is done by assigning commands to variables using the backquotes and the variable is used instead of the command. Variable substitution enables the programmer to work on the value of the variable based on its state.

263: What are the file test operators in shell?

Answer:

The file test operators in shell are used to check the files for specific properties. Here are some:

a) -b <filename> returns TRUE if the file is a block special file
b) -c <filename> returns TRUE if the file is a character file special
c) -d <filename> returns TRUE if it is a directory
d) -f <filename> returns TRUE if it is a normal file
e) -r <filename> returns TRUE if it has readable permission
f) -w <filename> returns TRUE if it has writable permission
g) -x <filename> returns TRUE if it has executable permission
h) -e<filename> returns TRUE if it exists either as a file or folder

264: How will you solve the arithmetic expressions in UNIX?

Answer:

a) Using *expr* with values

   Example:

   echo 'expr 3 + 9'

b) Using *expr* with variables

   Example:

   echo 'expr $p + $q '

265: How will you use Boolean operators?

Answer:

a) 'Logical and ' i.e. 'a'. Returns true, if both conditions are satisfied else, false

   Example:

Operators and Shell Substitutions 127

[$p –lt 8 –a $q –lt 13]

b) 'Logical or' i.e. 'o'. Returns true,

c) if any one condition is satisfied

Example:

[$p –lt 8 –o $q –lt 13]

266: How will you check the size of a string?
Answer:

a) '-z'. Returns true, if the operand size is zero

Example:

[-z $my_strvar1]

b) '-n'. Returns true, if the operand size is non - zero

267: What is the use of '-u' and '-g'?
Answer:

a) '-u': If the 'SGID' (Set Group id) of a file is enabled, returns true else, false

Example:

[-u $my_file3]

b) '-g': If the 'SUID' (Set User id) of a file is enabled, returns true else, false

Example:

[-g $my_file3]

268: How will you check the access of a file?
Answer:

The ways to check the access of a file are:

a) Using '-r'. If the file is readable, returns true else, returns false

Example:

-r $my_filename1 //returns true or false

b) Using '-w'. If the file writable, returns true else returns false

Example:

-w $my_filename1 //returns true or false

269: How will you use escape sequence in echo command?

Answer:

We can use escape sequence in *echo* command using '-e'. To substitute the escape sequence in the statement '-e' is used. To disable the substitution of escape sequence, '-E' is used.

Example:

my_var2=32

echo –e "value of myvar2 is $my_var2 \n"

270: What is called command substitution?

Answer:

Substituting the output of the command to the assigned variable is called command substitution.

Example:

My_var_date2=`date`

271: How will you substitute a name for a variable using ':+'?

Answer:

my_var2="Helllo"

Operators and Shell Substitutions 129

echo${my_var2:+ "my_value"} #my_value

echo "$my_var2" #Helllo

If *my_var2* is set, '*my_value*' will be used i.e. substituted for '*my_var2*'. The value of the '*my_var2*' does not change.

272: How will you substitute a name for a variable using ':-'?
Answer:

unset my_var2

echo ${my_var2:- "my_value"} #my_value

echo "$my_var2" # nothing will be displayed

If *my_var2* is unset/null, '*my_value*' will be used i.e. substituted for '*my_var2*'. The value of the 'my_var2' does not change.

273: How will you set a value to unset/null variable?
Answer:

We can set the value to unset/null variable using ':='

Example:

unset my_var2

echo ${my_var2:="my_value"} #my_value

echo "$my_var2" #my_value

274: What is 'Here' document?
Answer:

'Here' document provides an interactive program by giving required input without the user.

Example:

cat<<Helllo

aaaaaaaaaaaaaa

bbbbbbbbbbbb

Helllo

Cat - command

Helllo - delimeter

275: How will you discard the output of a command?

Answer:

We can discard the output of a command by redirecting the output to the file *'dev/null'*. This file discards all its input automatically.

Example:

date>special_file _name

date - command

special_file_name - dev/null

276: How will you delete a function?

Answer:

We can delete a function using '*.f'*

Example:

$unset .f my_functionname2

The function *'my_functionname2'* will be removed from the shell.

HR Interview Questions

Review these typical interview questions and think about how you would answer them. Read the answers listed; you will find best possible answers along with strategies and suggestions

1: Where do you find ideas?

Answer:

Ideas can come from all places, and an interviewer wants to see that your ideas are just as varied. Mention multiple places that you gain ideas from, or settings in which you find yourself brainstorming. Additionally, elaborate on how you record ideas or expand upon them later.

2: How do you achieve creativity in the workplace?

Answer:

It's important to show the interviewer that you're capable of being resourceful and innovative in the workplace, without stepping outside the lines of company values. Explain where ideas normally stem from for you (examples may include an exercise such as list-making or a mind map), and connect this to a particular task in your job that it would be helpful to be creative in.

3: How do you push others to create ideas?

Answer:

If you're in a supervisory position, this may be requiring employees to submit a particular number of ideas, or to complete regular idea-generating exercises, in order to work their creative muscles. However, you can also push others around you to create ideas simply by creating more of your own. Additionally, discuss with the interviewer the importance of questioning people as a way to inspire ideas and change.

4: Describe your creativity.

Answer:

Try to keep this answer within the professional realm, but if you have an impressive background in something creative outside of your employment history, don't be afraid to include it in your answer also. The best answers about creativity will relate problem-solving skills, goal-setting, and finding innovative ways to tackle a project or make a sale in the workplace. However, passions outside of the office are great, too (so long as they don't cut into your work time or mental space).

5: How would you handle a negative coworker?

Answer:

Everyone has to deal with negative coworkers – and the single best way to do so is to remain positive. You may try to build a relationship with the coworker or relate to them in some way, but even if your efforts are met with a cold shoulder, you must retain your positive attitude. Above all, stress that you would never allow a coworker's negativity to impact your own work or productivity.

6: What would you do if you witnessed a coworker surfing the web, reading a book, etc, wasting company time?

Answer:

The interviewer will want to see that you realize how detrimental it is for employees to waste company time, and that it is not something you take lightly. Explain the way you would adhere to company policy, whether that includes talking to the coworker yourself, reporting the behavior straight to a supervisor, or talking to someone in HR.

7: How do you handle competition among yourself and other employees?

Answer:

Healthy competition can be a great thing, and it is best to stay focused on the positive aspects of this here. Don't bring up conflict among yourself and other coworkers, and instead focus on the motivation to keep up with the great work of others, and the ways in which coworkers may be a great support network in helping to push you to new successes.

8: When is it okay to socialize with coworkers?

Answer:

This question has two extreme answers (all the time, or never), and your interviewer, in most cases, will want to see that you fall somewhere in the middle. It's important to establish solid relationships with your coworkers, but never at the expense of getting work done. Ideally, relationship-building can happen with exercises of teamwork and special projects, as well as in the break room.

9: Tell me about a time when a major change was made at your last job, and how you handled it.

Answer:

Provide a set-up for the situation including the old system, what the change was, how it was implemented, and the results of the change, and include how you felt about each step of the way. Be sure that your initial thoughts on the old system are neutral, and that your excitement level grows with each step of the new change, as an interviewer will be pleased to see your adaptability.

10: When delegating tasks, how do you choose which tasks go to which team members?

Answer:

The interviewer is looking to gain insight into your thought process with this question, so be sure to offer thorough reasoning behind your choice. Explain that you delegate tasks based on each individual's personal strengths, or that you look at how many other projects each person is working on at the time, in order to create the best fit possible.

11: Tell me about a time when you had to stand up for something you believed strongly about to coworkers or a supervisor.

Answer:

While it may be difficult to explain a situation of conflict to an interviewer, this is a great opportunity to display your passions and convictions, and your dedication to your beliefs. Explain not just the situation to the interviewer, but also elaborate on why it was so important to you to stand up for the issue, and how your coworker or supervisor responded to you afterward – were they more respectful? Unreceptive? Open-minded? Apologetic?

12: Tell me about a time when you helped someone finish their work, even though it wasn't "your job."

Answer:

Though you may be frustrated when required to pick up someone else's slack, it's important that you remain positive about lending a hand. The interviewer will be looking to see if you're a team player, and by helping someone else finish a task that he or she couldn't manage alone, you show both your willingness to help the team succeed, and your own competence.

13 What are the challenges of working on a team? How do you handle this?

Answer:

There are many obvious challenges to working on a team, such as handling different perspectives, navigating individual schedules, or accommodating difficult workers. It's best to focus on one challenge, such as individual team members missing deadlines or failing to keep commitments, and then offer a solution that clearly addresses the problem. For example, you could organize weekly status meetings for your team to discuss progress or assign shorter deadlines in order to keep the long-term deadline on schedule.

14: Do you value diversity in the workplace?

Answer:

Diversity is important in the workplace in order to foster an environment that is accepting, equalizing, and full of different perspectives and backgrounds. Be sure to show your awareness of these issues and stress the importance of learning from others' experiences.

15: How would you handle a situation in which a coworker was not accepting of someone else's diversity?

Answer:

Explain that it is important to adhere to company policies regarding diversity, and that you would talk to the relevant supervisors or management team. When it is appropriate, it could also be best to talk to the coworker in question about the benefits of alternate perspectives – if you can handle the situation yourself, it's best not to bring resolvable issues to management.

16: Are you rewarded more from working on a team, or accomplishing a task on your own?

Answer:

It's best to show a balance between these two aspects – your employer wants to see that you're comfortable working on your own, and that you can complete tasks efficiently and well without assistance. However, it's also important for your employer to see that you can be a team player, and that you understand the value that multiple perspectives and efforts can bring to a project.

17: Tell me about a time when you didn't meet a deadline.

Answer:

Ideally, this hasn't happened – but if it has, make sure you use a minor example to illustrate the situation, emphasize how long ago it happened, and be sure that you did as much as you could to ensure that the deadline was met. Additionally, be sure to include what you learned about managing time better or prioritizing tasks in order to meet all future deadlines.

18: How do you eliminate distractions while working?

Answer:

With the increase of technology and the ease of communication, new distractions arise every day. Your interviewer will want to see that you are still able to focus on work, and that your productivity has not been affected, by an example showing a routine you employ in order to stay on task.

19: Tell me about a time when you worked in a position with a weekly or monthly quota to meet. How often were you successful?

Answer:

Your numbers will speak for themselves, and you must answer this question honestly. If you were regularly met your quotas, be sure to highlight this in a confident manner and don't be shy in pointing out your strengths in this area. If your statistics are less than stellar, try to point out trends in which they increased toward the end of your employment, and show reflection as to ways you can improve in the future.

20: Tell me about a time when you met a tough deadline, and how you were able to complete it.

Answer:

Explain how you were able to prioritize tasks, or to delegate portions of an assignments to other team members, in order to deal with a tough deadline. It may be beneficial to specify why the deadline was tough – make sure it's clear that it was not a result of procrastination on your part. Finally, explain how you were able to successfully meet the deadline, and what it took to get there in the end.

21: How do you stay organized when you have multiple projects on your plate?

Answer:

The interviewer will be looking to see that you can manage your time and work well – and being able to handle multiple projects at once, and still giving each the attention it deserves, is a great mark of a worker's competence and efficiency. Go through a typical process of goal-setting and prioritizing, and explain the steps of these to the interviewer, so he or she can see how well you manage time.

22: How much time during your work day do you spend on "auto-pilot?"

Answer:

While you may wonder if the employer is looking to see how efficient you are with this question (for example, so good at your job that you don't have to think about it), but in almost every case, the employer wants to see that you're constantly thinking, analyzing, and processing what's going on in the workplace. Even if things are running smoothly, there's usually an opportunity somewhere to make things more efficient or to increase sales or productivity. Stress your dedication to ongoing development and convey that being on "auto-pilot" is not conducive to that type of success.

23: How do you handle deadlines?

Answer:

The most important part of handling tough deadlines is to prioritize tasks and set goals for completion, as well as to delegate or eliminate unnecessary work. Lead the interviewer through a general scenario and display your competency through your ability to organize and set priorities, and most importantly, remain calm.

24: Tell me about your personal problem-solving process.

Answer:

Your personal problem-solving process should include outlining the problem, coming up with possible ways to fix the problem, and setting a clear action plan that leads to resolution. Keep your answer brief and organized, and explain the steps in a concise, calm manner that shows you are level-headed even under stress.

25: What sort of things at work can make you stressed?

Answer:

As it's best to stay away from negatives, keep this answer brief and simple. While answering that nothing at work makes you stressed will not be very believable to the interviewer, keep your answer to one generic principle such as when members of a team don't keep their commitments, and then focus on a solution you generally employ to tackle that stress, such as having weekly status meetings or intermittent deadlines along the course of a project.

26: What do you look like when you are stressed about something? How do you solve it?

Answer:

This is a trick question – your interviewer wants to hear that you don't look any different when you're stressed, and that you don't allow negative emotions to interfere with your productivity. As far as how you solve your stress, it's best if you have a simple solution mastered, such as simply taking deep breaths and counting to 10 to bring yourself back to the task at hand.

27: Can you multi-task?

Answer:

Some people can, and some people can't. The most important part of multi-tasking is to keep a clear head at all times about what needs to be done, and what priority each task falls under. Explain how you evaluate tasks to determine priority, and how you manage your time in order to ensure that all are completed efficiently.

28: How many hours per week do you work?

Answer:

Many people get tricked by this question, thinking that answering more hours is better – however, this may cause an employer to wonder why you have to work so many hours in order to get the work done that other people can do in a shorter amount of time. Give a fair estimate of hours that it should take you to complete a job and explain that you are also willing to work extra whenever needed.

29: How many times per day do you check your email?

Answer:

While an employer wants to see that you are plugged into modern technology, it is also important that the number of times you check your email per day is relatively low – perhaps two to three times per day (dependent on the specific field you're in). Checking email is often a great distraction in the workplace, and while it is important to remain connected, much correspondence can simply be handled together in the morning and afternoon.

30: How do you make decisions?

Answer:

This is a great opportunity for you to wow your interviewer with your decisiveness, confidence, and organizational skills. Make sure that you outline a process for decision-making, and that you stress the importance of weighing your options, as well as in trusting intuition. If you answer this question skillfully and with ease, your interviewer will trust in your capability as a worker.

31: What are the most difficult decisions for you to make?

Answer:

Explain your relationship to decision-making, and a general synopsis of the process you take in making choices. If there is a particular type of decision that you often struggle with, such as those that involve other people, make sure to explain why that type of decision is tough for you, and how you are currently engaged in improving your skills.

32: When making a tough decision, how do you gather information?

Answer:

If you're making a tough choice, it's best to gather information from as many sources as possible. Lead the interviewer through your process of taking information from people in different areas, starting first with advice from experts in your field, feedback from coworkers or other clients, and by looking analytically at your own past experiences.

33: Tell me about a decision you made that did not turn out well.

Answer:

Honesty and transparency are great values that your interviewer will appreciate – outline the choice you made, why you made it, the results of your poor decision – and finally (and most importantly!) what you learned from the decision. Give the interviewer reason to trust that you wouldn't make a decision like that again in the future.

34: Are you able to make decisions quickly?

Answer:

You may be able to make decisions quickly but be sure to communicate your skill in making sound, thorough decisions as well. Discuss the importance of making a decision quickly, and how you do so, as well as the necessity for each decision to first be well-informed

35: What is the best way for a company to advertise?

Answer:

If you're going for a position in any career other than marketing, this question is probably intended to demonstrate your ability to think critically and to provide reflective support for your answers. As such, the particular method you choose is not so important as why you've chosen it. For example, word of mouth advertising is important because customers will inherently trust the source, and social media advertising is important as it reaches new customers quickly and cheaply.

36: Is it better to gain a new customer or to keep an old one?

Answer:

In almost every case, it is better to keep an old customer, and it's important that you are able to articulate why this is. First, new customers generally cost companies more than retaining old ones does, and new customers are more likely to switch to a different company. Additionally, keeping old customers is a great way to provide a stable backbone for the company, as well as to also gain new customers as they are likely to recommend your company to friends.

37: What is the best way to win clients from competitors?

Answer:

There are many schools of thought on the best way to win clients from competitors, and unless you know that your interviewer adheres to a specific thought or practice, it's best to keep this question general. Rather than using absolute language, focus on the benefits of one or two strategies and show a clear, critical understanding of how these ways can succeed in a practical application.

38: How do you feel about companies monitoring internet usage?

Answer:

Generally speaking, most companies will monitor some degree of internet usage over their employees – and during an interview is not the best time to rebel against this practice. Instead, focus on positive aspects such as the way it can lead to increased productivity for some employees who may be easily lost in the world of resourceful information available to them.

39: What is your first impression of our company?

Answer:

Obviously, this should be a positive answer! Pick out a couple key components of the company's message or goals that you especially identify with or that pertain to your experience and discuss why you believe these missions are so important.

40: Tell me about your personal philosophy on business.

Answer:

Your personal philosophy on business should be well-thought out, and in line with the missions and objectives of the company. Stay focused on positive aspects such as the service it can provide, and the lessons people gain in business, and offer insight as to where your philosophy has come from.

41: What's most important in a business model: sales, customer service, marketing, management, etc.?

Answer:

For many positions, it may be a good strategy to tailor this answer to the type of field you're working in, and to explain why that aspect of business is key. However, by explaining that each aspect is integral to the function as a whole, you can display a greater sense of business savvy to the interviewer and may stand out in his or her mind as a particularly aware candidate.

42: How do you keep up with news and emerging trends in the field?

Answer:

The interviewer wants to see that you are aware of what's

currently going on in your field. It is important that your education does not stop after college, and the most successful candidates will have a list of resources they regularly turn to already in place, so that they may stay aware and engaged in developing trends.

43: Would you have a problem adhering to company policies on social media?

Answer:

Social media concerns in the workplace have become a greater issue, and many companies now outline policies for the use of social media. Interviewers will want to be assured that you won't have a problem adhering to company standards, and that you will maintain a consistent, professional image both in the office and online.

44: Tell me about one of the greatest problems facing X industry today.

Answer:

If you're involved in your career field and spend time on your own studying trends and new developments, you should be able to display an awareness of both problems and potential solutions coming up in the industry. Research some of the latest news before heading into the interview and be prepared to discuss current events thoroughly.

45: What do you think it takes to be successful in our company?

Answer:

Research the company prior to the interview. Be aware of the company's mission and main objectives, as well as some of the biggest names in the company, and also keep in mind how they achieved success. Keep your answer focused on specific objectives you could reach in order to help the company achieve its goals.

46: What is your favorite part of working in this career field?

Answer:

This question is an opportunity to discuss some of your favorite aspects of the job, and to highlight why you are a great candidate for the particular position. Choose elements of the work you enjoy that are related to what you would do if hired for the position. Remember to remain enthusiastic and excited for the opportunities you could attain in the job.

47: What do you see happening to your career in the next 10 years?

Answer:

If you're plugged in to what's happening in your career now and are making an effort to stay abreast of emerging trends in your field, you should be able to offer the interviewer several predictions as to where your career or field may be heading. This insight and level of awareness shows a level of dedication and interest that is important to employers.

48: What are the three most important things you're looking for in a position?

Answer:

The top three things you want in a position should be similar to the top three things the employer wants from an employee, so that it is clear that you are well-matched to the job. For example, the employer wants a candidate who is well-qualified for and has practical experience – and you want a position that allows you to use your education and skills to their best applications. The employer wants a candidate who is willing to take on new challenges and develop new systems to increase sales or productivity – and you want a position that pushes you and offers opportunities to develop, create, and lead new initiatives. The employer wants a candidate who will grow into and stay with the company for a long time – and you want a position that offers stability and believes in building a strong team. Research what the employer is looking for beforehand and match your objectives to theirs.

49: How are you evaluating the companies you're looking to work with?

Answer:

While you may feel uncomfortable exerting your own requirements during the interview, the employer wants to see that you are thinking critically about the companies you're applying with, just as they are critically looking at you. Don't be afraid to specify what your needs from a company are (but do try to make sure they match up well with the company – preferably before you apply there and show confidence and decisiveness in your answer. The interviewer wants to know that you're the kind of person who knows what they want, and how to get it.

50: Are you comfortable working for _____ salary?

Answer:

If the answer to this question is no, it may be a bit of a deal-breaker in a first interview, as you are unlikely to have much room to negotiate. You can try to leverage a bit by highlighting specific experience you have, and how that makes you qualified for more, but be aware that this is very difficult to navigate at this step of the process. To avoid this situation, be aware of industry standards and, if possible, company standards, prior to your application.

51: Why did you choose your last job?

Answer:

In learning what led you to your last job, the interviewer is able to get a feel for the types of things that motivate you. Keep these professionally-focused and remain passionate about the early points of your career, and how excited you were to get started in the field.

52: How long has it been since your last job and why?

Answer:

Be sure to have an explanation prepared for all gaps in employment, and make sure it's a professional reason. Don't mention difficulties you may have had in finding a job, and instead focus on positive things such as pursuing outside interests or perhaps returning to school for additional education.

53: What other types of jobs have you been looking for?

Answer:

The answer to this question can show the interviewer that you're both on the market and in demand. Mention jobs you've applied for or looked at that are closely related to your field, or similar to the position you're interviewing for. Don't bring up last-ditch efforts that found you applying for a part-time job completely unrelated to your field.

54: Have you ever been disciplined at work?

Answer:

Hopefully the answer here is no – but if you have been disciplined for something at work though, be absolutely sure that you can explain it thoroughly. Detail what you learned from the situation and reflect on how you grew after the process.

55: What is your availability like?

Answer:

Your availability should obviously be as open as possible, and any gaps in availability should be explained and accounted for. Avoid asking about vacation or personal days (as well as other benefits and convey to the interviewer how serious you are about your work.

56: May I contact your current employer?

Answer:

If possible, it is best to allow an interviewer to contact your current employer as a reference. However, if it's important that your employer is not contacted, explain your reason tactfully, such as you just started job searching and you haven't had the opportunity yet to inform them that you are looking for other employment. Be careful of this reasoning though, as employers may wonder if you'll start shopping for something better while employed with them as well.

facebook.com/vibrantpublishers

57: Do you have any valuable contacts you could bring to our business?

Answer:

It's great if you can bring knowledge, references, or other contacts that your new employer may be able to network with. However, be sure that you aren't offering up any of your previous employer's clients, or in any way violating contractual agreements.

58: How soon would you be available to start working?

Answer:

While you want to be sure that you're available to start as soon as possible if the company is interested in hiring you, if you still have another job, be sure to give them at least two weeks' notice. Though your new employer may be anxious for you to start, they will want to hire a worker whom they can respect for giving adequate notice, so that they won't have to worry if you'll eventually leave them in the lurch.

59: Why would your last employer say that you left?

Answer:

The key to this question is that your employer's answer must be the same as your own answer about why you left. For instance, if you've told your employer that you left to find a position with greater opportunities for career advancement, your employer had better not say that you were let go for missing too many days of work. Honesty is key in your job application process.

60: How long have you been actively looking for a job?

Answer:

It's best if you haven't been actively looking for a job for very long, as a long period of time may make the interviewer wonder why no one else has hired you. If it has been awhile, make sure to explain why, and keep it positive. Perhaps you haven't come across many opportunities that provide you with enough of a challenge or that are adequately matched to someone of your education and experience.

61: When don't you show up to work?

Answer:

Clearly, the only time acceptable to miss work is for a real emergency or when you're truly sick – so don't start bringing up times now that you plan to miss work due to vacations or family birthdays. Alternatively, you can tell the interviewer how dedicated to your work you are, and how you always strive to be fully present and to put in the same amount of work every time you come in, even when you're feeling slightly under the weather.

62: What is the most common reason you miss work?

Answer:

If there is a reason that you will miss work routinely, this is the time to disclose it – but doing so during an interview will reflect negatively on you. Ideally, you will only miss work during cases of extreme illness or other emergencies.

63: What is your attendance record like?

Answer:

Be sure to answer this question honestly, but ideally you will have already put in the work to back up the fact that you rarely miss days or arrive late. However, if there are gaps in your attendance, explain them briefly with appropriate reasons, and make sure to emphasize your dedication to your work, and reliability.

64: Where did you hear about this position?

Answer:

This may seem like a simple question, but the answer can actually speak volumes about you. If you were referred by a friend or another employee who works for the company, this is a great chance to mention your connection (if the person is in good standing!). However, if you heard about it from somewhere like a career fair or a work placement agency, you may want to focus on how pleased you were to come across such a wonderful opportunity.

65: Tell me anything else you'd like me to know when making a hiring decision.

Answer:

This is a great opportunity for you to give a final sell of yourself to the interviewer – use this time to remind the interviewer of why you are qualified for the position, and what you can bring to the company that no one else can. Express your excitement for the opportunity to work with a company pursuing X mission.

66: Why would your skills be a good match with X objective of our company?

Answer:

If you've researched the company before the interview, answering this question should be no problem. Determine several of the company's main objectives and explain how specific skills that you have are conducive to them. Also, think about ways that your experience and skills can translate to helping the company expand upon these objectives, and to reach further goals. If your old company had a similar objective, give a specific example of how you helped the company to meet it.

67: What do you think this job entails?

Answer:

Make sure you've researched the position well before heading into the interview. Read any and all job descriptions you can find (at best, directly from the employer's website or job posting), and make note of key duties, responsibilities, and experience required. Few things are less impressive to an interviewer than a candidate who has no idea what sort of job they're actually being interviewed for.

68: Is there anything else about the job or company you'd like to know?

Answer:

If you have learned about the company beforehand, this is a great opportunity to show that you put in the effort to study before the interview. Ask questions about the company's mission in relation to current industry trends, and engage the interviewer in interesting, relevant conversation. Additionally, clear up anything else you need to know about the specific position before leaving – so that if the interviewer calls with an offer, you'll be prepared to answer.

69: Are you the best candidate for this position?

Answer:

Yes! Offer specific details about what makes you qualified for this position and be sure to discuss (and show) your unbridled passion and enthusiasm for the new opportunity, the job, and the company.

70: How did you prepare for this interview?

Answer:

The key part of this question is to make sure that you have prepared! Be sure that you've researched the company, their objectives, and their services prior to the interview, and know as much about the specific position as you possibly can. It's also helpful to learn about the company's history and key players in the current organization.

71: If you were hired here, what would you do on your first day?

Answer:

While many people will answer this question in a boring fashion, going through the standard first day procedures, this question is actually a great chance for you to show the interviewer why you will make a great hire. In addition to things like going through training or orientation, emphasize how much you would enjoy meeting your supervisors and coworkers, or how you would spend a lot of the day asking questions and taking in all of your new surroundings.

72: Have you viewed our company's website?

Answer:

Clearly, you should have viewed the company's website and done some preliminary research on them before coming to the interview. If for some reason you did not, do not say that you did, as the interviewer may reveal you by asking a specific question about it. If you did look at the company's website, this is an appropriate time to bring up something you saw there that was of particular interest to you, or a value that you especially supported.

73: How does X experience on your resume relate to this position?

Answer:

Many applicants will have some bit of experience on their resume that does not clearly translate to the specific job in question. However, be prepared to be asked about this type of seemingly-irrelevant experience, and have a response prepared that takes into account similar skill sets or training that the two may share.

74: Why do you want this position?

Answer:

Keep this answer focused positively on aspects of this specific job that will allow you to further your skills, offer new experience, or that will be an opportunity for you to do something that you particularly enjoy. Don't tell the interviewer that you've been looking for a job for a long time, or that the pay is very appealing, or you will appear unmotivated and opportunistic.

75: How is your background relevant to this position?

Answer:

Ideally, this should be obvious from your resume. However, in instances where your experience is more loosely-related to the position, make sure that you've researched the job and company well before the interview. That way, you can intelligently relate the experience and skills that you do have, to similar skills that would be needed in the new position. Explain specifically how your skills will translate and use words to describe your background such as "preparation" and "learning." Your prospective position should be described as an "opportunity" and a chance for "growth and development."

76: How do you feel about X mission of our company?

Answer:

It's important to have researched the company prior to the interview – and if you've done so, this question won't catch you off guard. The best answer is one that is simple, to the point, and shows knowledge of the mission at hand. Offer a few short statements as to why you believe in the mission's importance and note that you would be interested in the chance to work with a company that supports it.

INDEX

UNIX Shell Programming Interview Questions

C Shell – Beginner

1: What must you do before you are able to run your new script for the first time by its name or with an alias?
2: The following command is included in the .login script of a user:
3: If the condition If (-r filename) fails (returns false), what are the possible reasons?
4: Which is the difference between the next two statements?
5: Given the code snippet:
6: What will the output of the following commands be? Explain.
7: What does the command rehash do?
8: How could you ensure that a script will be run in *csh*?
9: Given that script1 is an executable C shell script situated in *directory* /home/myhomedir/project1/data/dir1, use three ways to run it, explaining the pros and cons.
10: What will be the value of the sixrem variable, after executing this command?
11: Name two ways to obtain the length of a string, giving a simple example for each one.
12: Create a script that displays a list of regular files from the current directory.
13: Describe in short, the word-completion feature of the *tcsh* shell.
14: In *tcsh*, how are the remaining choices (if any) listed whenever the word completion fails?
15: In *tcsh*, how do you disable filename substitution?
16: Compare the *schedtcsh* built-in command with the UNIX/Linux at command.
17: Schedule a *prompt* change at 10:55 as a reminder for an oncoming event.

INDEX

18: What is the impact of *-f* option in the first line of a *csh* script?
19: How can you start a job in the background, and then terminate your login session, without terminating the background job?
20: Which is the difference between *echo c{1,4,2,5,1}* and *echo [c]{1,4,2,5,1}*?
21: Display the first and last arguments of a script, regardless of the number of arguments, and without a loop.
22: How will you set the 'search path' in *csv*?
23: Create a tar archive into /home/user1/myarch.tar, including all files ending in .c, .h, .l, .y, .o and .cc and also the *Makefile* from two directories, ~/dir1 and ~/dir2.
24: Your script must be executed with exactly two arguments, otherwise would be terminated. Write a code to implement these checks.
25: Write a pipeline that reads from the *j-th* line up to the *k-th* line of a text file, without using *awk*.

C Shell – Intermediate

26: Explain the following commands:
27: How could you move cursor to specified coordinates on screen? (*tcsh*)
28: What is the result of this loop?
29: Assuming there is a label cleanup somewhere in a script, explain the command *onintr cleanup*
30: Is there a way to repeat a command for a predefined number of times, without using a counter-controlled loop?
31: *csh* and *tcsh* both support the filename & command completion feature. But the feature works differently in *csh* than in *tcsh*. Name the differences.
32: Name the special login files for *csh* and *tcsh* in the order used by each shell.
33: What do the following lines do? Explain the differences.
34: You can run a script by its name, using an alias or using source. Explain the differences in using each of the three methods. When is it suitable to use each method?
35: How could you override a defined alias? Give a simple example.

www.vibrantpublishers.com

36: You plan to write a script that will process the file passed to it as the only argument on the command line. So, your script must accept at least one argument and this single or first argument must be an existing file. Write the necessary checks, displaying the appropriate messages.

37: Write a code excerpt that processes (here, just displays) the elements of an array, from the first one to the last one.

38: Complete the last echo command with a descriptive message in the following script. In other words, explain the value of pct variable.

39: Extract just the mode of a given file, using two different ways.

40: Which is the output of the following excerpt?

41: Find the position of a substring in a given string. Display a message if the string does not contain this substring.

42: Change the case of a string.

43: Assume that in a script the value of a variable *limt* becomes equal to 92.1. Display the message:

44: Suppose a script contains the following snippet.

45: Create a script that converts the filenames from current directory to lower case letters.

46: Name some basic differences between *csh* and *tcsh*.

47: Compare the *tcsh* shell variables *correct* and *autocorrect*.

48: What is the purpose of the special alias shell?

49: Which is the method to bind the keys to the standard *vi* or *emacs* bindings?

50: Which is the purpose of shell's variable *color*?

51: Set your prompt to display *username@hostname: pwd>*

52: How can you start (from shell prompt) 2 commands "in the background", ensuring that the second command will start after the completion of the first one?

53: Write a script to display a sorted listing of the unique words in a text file.

54: Display the value of your PATH variable with each path in a separate line.

55: Why the inclusion of a dot (.) in a search path is not a good practice?

56: Explain the logical expression @ $x = (\$n < 5 \;||\; 20 <= \$n)$ and then also write the negation of this expression.

INDEX

57: What are the differences between the below given two commands and when can we use both of them?
58: Explain this small script:
59: A script prompts the user to type in something, using the following syntax:

C Shell – Advanced

60: Explain local vs environment variables.
61: Explain Searchpath.
62: Explain Globbing.
63: Fix the following switch statement, explaining your corrections.
64: Name some basic differences between *bash* and *csh* syntax and/or features.
65: Suggest a way to overcome lack of functions in C shells.
66: From */tmp* directory, issue (*cd ; pwd*) ; *pwd*. Explain the performed actions and the output.
67: Write a code excerpt that prompts for a filename, reads the user input, checks if this is a regular file and if so, stores it in an array for further processing. The procedure must be repeated until the user hits the Enter key.
68: Use *awk* mathematical functions to calculate the area of a circle (area = PI*rad2)
69: Use *awk*in order to split an entry from */etc/passwd* file into an array, replacing the password field with the string *"secret"*.
70: Explain the following snippet.
71: Name the available ways (with examples) to replace any occurrence of a substring with another substring in a string.
72: Write a snippet to categorize the files from a directory, based on their extension (for simplicity, take care only for *.c, .o, .txt,* and *.png files*).
73: Write a script that will display a menu of choices to the user. The menu should be displayed over and over, until the user will select the specific "exit" option. The script should give to the user the following options:
74: Create a script that will be run automatically when the user logs into the system, and send a mail message to the user, if the total number of aliases on his *.cshrc* file are greater than a threshold (let's say 40).

75: Display the filenames and permissions of each file in your current directory.
76: Create a script that creates a list of all file systems (mount points) on the current system and the current percent used.
77: Explain the following script and suggest any enhancements.
78: Use the *bc* calculator in order to do a variable comparison involving floating-point numbers. Write your example as part of an if conditional statement.
79: Write a while loop using a floating-point comparison statement as the loop condition (and loop control).
80: If there is no simple file reading facility in the C-shell, what could you use to tide this over?
81: Extract the n-th line of a text file and assign it in a variable.
82: Assuming that *input_file* is a text file with space-separated fields, what will be the value of *ncol* when the following command will be executed?
83: Find the minimum of the integer numbers that are stored in an array.
84: Explain the following block of commands:
85: The C shell provides one way to read a line:
86: Explain the following snippet.
87: Fix any syntax or logical error in the following script.
88: Explain this script.
89: Are there any differences between the next two commands?
90: Explain the following code block.
91: Suppose that you have a contacts file in the format (no headers line):
92: Which is the valid syntax of *getopt* command in a C shell?
93: Explain in short the following script:
94: Write a script which calculates the min, max and average of a set of floating-point numbers, stored in an array.
95: You have an input data file with a symmetrical schema (the same number of fields in each record) where the first line contains the headings of the fields. You want to extract the 3rd column (field) of the actual data records, that is, of each record except the headers line (1st line) and any comment lines (assume that they begin with # or *). Give a solution and explain it in short.

INDEX

96: Suppose that *input_file* is a tabular data file with an asymmetric schema, that is, each record (line) may have different number of fields, and that the first 3 lines describe the used schema. Explain the following excerpt:

97: Suppose you have a data file but its internal format does not remain consistent. You want to extract two columns from this file, but you don't know the order of the columns, know only their headers: Name, and email.

98: Create a script to read a textfile line by line, to the end of the file. Do not use *awk*.

99: What is a limitation in options handling in C shells?

100: Rewrite the next script, using a more readable and clear logic.

Bash – Beginner

101: What is shebang?

102: What are pipes?

103: What is exit status?

104: What is a subshell? How do you create it?

105: Consider the following message:

106: The case statement is useful for comparing the value of a variable against a list of possible matches. True or false?

107: You don't remember the correct option (switch) for sort command, in order to sort some entries in reverse order. What could you do?

108: The first line of a shell script is:

109: You need to find all files under your */home* directory that were not accessed during last 10 days. What could you do?

110: How could you check if there are running *sshd* processes on your system?

111: What happens when you run the following command?

112: The next line is the beginning of a conditional statement in a bash script:

113: A for loop requires an arguments list. This list can result from:

114: Given the following nested loops, which command would you use in place of command-to-process-file for the shell to execute the last *cat* command, if the test condition is met?

www.vibrantpublishers.com

115: What would happen if the following command was in the .bash_profile of a user?
116: The value of a variable should be compared against 8 possible values (and/or patterns) and some commands, different for each possible value, should be run. What is the structure that you would prefer for these checks?
117: What is the expected output from the following command?
118: How can you run a job in the background?
119: What is the action performed by the command *cd -*?
120: Which are the special meanings of character ~ for the bash shell?
121: What is the difference between *variable5* and *$variable5*?
122: What is defined with the command *variable=value*, a local or an environment variable?
123: How can you find the bash shell version that is installed on your system?
124: What does the bash built-in variable EDITOR do?
125: What is the purpose of shell built-in variable PATH?
126: Is there any way to declare an integer variable in bash?
127: How would the shell interpret the command "*echo ??a*"?

Bash – Intermediate

128: Write a simple script that will check the numeric UID of the user executing it, will display a message and then will exit, if the user is not root.
129: Construct a bash shell pattern to match any alphanumeric string ending with exactly one digit.
130: Write a command that lists the filenames that match the pattern *Name#_##* exactly.
131: Write a command to get the list of all directory entries (files & subdirectories) that start with . (dot), except . (dot) and .. (double dot).
132: You must check if a certain file exists on your system and if you have read access to it. Which syntax will you use?
133: Consider the following snippet.
134: What happens when you run this loop?

INDEX

135: What happens when you run this loop?

136: You should find the entry that defines user account *dbuser1* from the *passwd* file.

137: Use the correct syntax to display all lines from the file named *datafile* that ends with the string *ing*. (a literal dot).

138: A configuration file of an application (or service) contains many lines that are commented out, and just two or three useful lines. How could you display only the essential (uncommented) data?

139: How can the shell pass variables into *awk*?

140: True or False: When input is provided to *awk*, *awk* will process every record.

141: True or False: All unquoted strings are treated as variables, keywords or functions in *awk* statements.

142: You have a simple (text) contacts file, containing lines in the following format:

143: True or False: In bash shell the array variables can be multi-dimensional.

144: How could you display the entire contents of an array variable?

145: How could you get the length (the total number of elements) of an array?

146: How could you initialize an array?

147: True or False: Array variables cannot be environment variables.

148: Is it possible to define a variable with local scope inside a function?

149: If you call a function using the syntax:

150: Is there any way to avoid overwriting the file when the following redirection syntax is used?

151: Explain the following syntax:

152: What is the result of the command?

153: Why is it preferable to use the TERM signal (-15) instead of the KILL signal (-9) in order to stop the execution of a process?

154: Is it possible to change the default behavior of the shell when it receives a certain signal?

155: What is the meaning of *$0* for an *awk* statement? What is the meaning of variables *$1, $2, ...* for the *awk*?

www.vibrantpublishers.com

156: Is it possible to define some actions to be performed before the processing of the input lines by the *awk* command?
157: Select all of the following that apply to bash shell variables. Explain all that do not apply.
158: True or False: A script invoked from the command line can export variables back to its parent shell.
159: Write the echo command which will display the following line, using " (double quotes).
160: How could you define your primary *prompt* to reflect the login name, the "at" sign, the system's hostname and the current working directory?
161: How can you set the value of a variable to the contents of a file?
162: What are the differences between the two forms of command substitution, $(*cmd*) and `*cmd*`?
163: Describe the "and" list execution.
164: Bash shell (version 4.2) permits representing and displaying characters in foreign alphabets. How? Give an example displaying the mathematical symbol PI.
165: Give the output of the following code snippet:
166: The permissions on a *directory* /*mydir* are *rw*-r---- and you are the owner of this directory. Can you display the contents of /*mydir*? Can you change directory to /*mydir*? Can you create a new file under /*mydir*? Can you read the contents of a file contained in /*mydir*?
167: Which are the two valid syntax forms to declare a function?
168: Correct the following function's declaration.
169: What does the += operator perform?

Bash – Advanced

170: Explain *whiptail*, *man* and *grep*.
171: Explain /*dev* and /*proc*.
172: Explain *trap* command.
173: What is POSIX?
174: Explain *tput* and *infocmp*.
175: What kind of problems would occur if you define a function named *ls*?

INDEX

176: Define a function named *pause_until_return*, to pause the execution of the script until the user presses the return key.

177: How can you create a functions library and what are the advantages of such a library?

178: Is it permissible to use recursive functions (functions that call themselves)?

179: The following code snippet uses a file descriptor in order to create a file:

180: If you should use an interactive command (like *sftp*) in a script, what could you use in order to automate this function (without user interaction)?

181: What is the output of the following?

182: What is the output of the following command?

183: Explain the following pipeline.

184: How could you declare an associative array?

185: Which syntax returns (expands to) the indexes in an array ARRAY?

186: What is the built-in *mapfile* command used for?

187: Write an equivalent but shorter form of the following if structure, without using if.

188: Give the output of the following snippet and explain it.

189: Set the positional parameters to a string then unset the positional parameters and then set them again to their original values.

190: The *rm* command just unlinks the file (*inode*) from the data blocks. To properly delete a file, it is required to overwrite the blocks occupied by the file. Create a script to securely delete the files passed to it as arguments.

191: Assuming there is a defined array named Array, what does this for loop do?

192: What is the impact of using the terminator characters ;;& and ;& in a case structure?

193: Write the output of the following case, assuming that 1) $1 equals to a, and 2) $1 equals to 5:

194: Name two ways to set an array to the contents of a text file.

195: Name a limitation of *getopts* bash built-in.

196: Debug the following script excerpt.

197: Debug the following script excerpt:
198: Write a script that replaces every occurrence of a pattern with another in a given file. The script receives 3 arguments: *pattern_to_be_replaced*
199: Create a function that capitalizes the first character of its string arguments.
200: What does the following code snippet do?
201: Describe the functionality of the following script.
202: Explain the following code snippet.
203: Which is the modern indirect reference form that is equivalent to the old one (*eval var1=\$$var2*)?
204: Explain this code snippet.
205: The following excerpt does not achieve to set the 3 variables (*my_var1, my_var2, my_var3*). Explain.
206: Write a script that recognizes and handles only the command options -l (followed by a value) and -m in any order. An invalid option will cause the script to terminate with an error, displaying the invalid option.
207: Give an example of downloading a URL using Bash shell.
208: Write the code to return a randomly selected index of an array (integer indexed), selecting a random element of the array.
209: Write a snippet to return a randomly selected string index of an associative array and the element associated with this index.
210: Name the obvious advantage of an "and" list.

Basics

211: What are the types of files used in UNIX?
212: Which type of file's name starts with '.'?
213: How will you display the file name starting with the particular letters say 'hel'?
214: Which characters are called meta-characters?
215: How does the interaction between user and UNIX system take place?
216: What is the purpose of '$'?
217: What is the purpose of '#'?
218: How will you know the functionality of a command in UNIX?

Commands

219: Explain the commands *getty* and *agetty*.
220: Explain strace and ltrace.
221: Explain the commands nice and pidof.
222: Explain lockfile.
223: Explain env.
224: Which command is used to list the hidden files in a directory?
225: How will you redirect the output to a file?
226: How will you search for a pattern in a file?
227: How will you append the output of a command to a file?
228: What is the purpose of '2>' in UNIX shell?
229: How will you get the output of a previous command as an input to the subsequent command?
230: Which commands are used to print the nth line of a file?
231: How will you search for a file in folders?
232: What is the purpose of '-r' and ''-v in grep command?
233: How will find a directory of a file?
234: How will you kill a process?
235: What are the ways to create a file?
236: What are the ways to get name of the cpu model?
237: How will you get the number of words in a file?

Variables and Arrays

238: What are positional parameters?
239: Explain the shift command.
240: Does = and -eq function similarly?
241: How will you initialize and print the values in UNIX?
242: How will you concatenate the variables in UNIX?
243: How will make the variable read-only?
244: How will you delete a variable?
245: What are the types of variables?
246: How will you get the file name and number of arguments accepted by the current script?

247: How will you get the status of the last executed command?
248: How will you achieve 'do-while' looping?
249: How will you call a function in UNIX?
250: What are the ways to get the process id of a shell?
251: How will you initialize an array?
252: How will you access the array variables?

Special Shell Variables

253: Explain the special shell variables.
254: How do you check if a string is empty with an operator?
255: Describe the purpose of 'killring('')'.
256: Describe the purpose of 'matchbeep('')'.
257: How will you list jobs?
258: Describe the purpose of 'correct('')'.
259: What are the functions of echo_style()?
260: How will you set the mode of the editor?
261: How will you avoid duplicate entries in the memory?

Operators and Shell Substitutions

262: What are the different types of substitutions available in Shell?
263: What are the file test operators in shell?
264: How will you solve the arithmetic expressions in UNIX?
265: How will you use Boolean operators?
266: How will you check the size of a string?
267: What is the use of '-u' and '-g'?
268: How will you check the access of a file?
269: How will you use escape sequence in echo command?
270: What is called command substitution?
271: How will you substitute a name for a variable using ':+'?
272: How will you substitute a name for a variable using ':-'?
273: How will you set a value to unset/null variable?
274: What is called 'Here Document'?
275: How will you discard the output of a command?

276: How will you delete a function?

HR Interview Questions

1: Where do you find ideas?
2: How do you achieve creativity in the workplace?
3: How do you push others to create ideas?
4: Describe your creativity.
5: How would you handle a negative coworker?
6: What would you do if you witnessed a coworker surfing the web, reading a book, etc, wasting company time?
7: How do you handle competition among yourself and other employees?
8: When is it okay to socialize with coworkers?
9: Tell me about a time when a major change was made at your last job, and how you handled it.
10: When delegating tasks, how do you choose which tasks go to which team members?
11: Tell me about a time when you had to stand up for something you believed strongly about to coworkers or a supervisor.
12: Tell me about a time when you helped someone finish their work, even though it wasn't "your job."
13: What are the challenges of working on a team? How do you handle this?
14: Do you value diversity in the workplace?
15: How would you handle a situation in which a coworker was not accepting of someone else's diversity?
16: Are you rewarded more from working on a team, or accomplishing a task on your own?
17: Tell me about a time when you didn't meet a deadline.
18: How do you eliminate distractions while working?
19: Tell me about a time when you worked in a position with a weekly or monthly quota to meet. How often were you successful?
20: Tell me about a time when you met a tough deadline, and how you were able to complete it.
21: How do you stay organized when you have multiple projects on your plate?
22: How much time during your work day do you spend on "auto-

pilot?"
23: How do you handle deadlines?
24: Tell me about your personal problem-solving process.
25: What sort of things at work can make you stressed?
26: What do you look like when you are stressed about something? How do you solve it?
27: Can you multi-task?
28: How many hours per week do you work?
29: How many times per day do you check your email?
30: How do you make decisions?
31: What are the most difficult decisions for you to make?
32: When making a tough decision, how do you gather information?
33: Tell me about a decision you made that did not turn out well.
34: Are you able to make decisions quickly?
35: What is the best way for a company to advertise?
36: Is it better to gain a new customer or to keep an old one?
37: What is the best way to win clients from competitors?
38: How do you feel about companies monitoring internet usage?
39: What is your first impression of our company?
40: Tell me about your personal philosophy on business.
41: What's most important in a business model: sales, customer service, marketing, management, etc.?
42: How do you keep up with news and emerging trends in the field?
43: Would you have a problem adhering to company policies on social media?
44: Tell me about one of the greatest problems facing X industry today.
45: What do you think it takes to be successful in our company?
46: What is your favorite part of working in this career field?
47: What do you see happening to your career in the next 10 years?
48: What are the three most important things you're looking for in a position?
49: How are you evaluating the companies you're looking to work with?
50: Are you comfortable working for _____ salary?

51: Why did you choose your last job?
52: How long has it been since your last job and why?
53: What other types of jobs have you been looking for?
54: Have you ever been disciplined at work?
55: What is your availability like?
56: May I contact your current employer?
57: Do you have any valuable contacts you could bring to our business?
58: How soon would you be available to start working?
59: Why would your last employer say that you left?
60: How long have you been actively looking for a job?
61: When don't you show up to work?
62: What is the most common reason you miss work?
63: What is your attendance record like?
64: Where did you hear about this position?
65: Tell me anything else you'd like me to know when making a hiring decision.
66: Why would your skills be a good match with X objective of our company?
67: What do you think this job entails?
68: Is there anything else about the job or company you'd like to know?
69: Are you the best candidate for this position?
70: How did you prepare for this interview?
71: If you were hired here, what would you do on your first day?
72: Have you viewed our company's website?
73: How does X experience on your resume relate to this position?
74: Why do you want this position?
75: How is your background relevant to this position?
76: How do you feel about X mission of our company?

Some of the following titles might also be handy:

1. NET Interview Questions You'll Most Likely Be Asked
2. Access VBA Programming Interview Questions You'll Most Likely Be Asked
3. Adobe ColdFusion Interview Questions You'll Most Likely Be Asked
4. Advanced C++ Interview Questions You'll Most Likely Be Asked
5. Advanced Excel Interview Questions You'll Most Likely Be Asked
6. Advanced JAVA Interview Questions You'll Most Likely Be Asked
7. Advanced SAS Interview Questions You'll Most Likely Be Asked
8. AJAX Interview Questions You'll Most Likely Be Asked
9. Algorithms Interview Questions You'll Most Likely Be Asked
10. Android Development Interview Questions You'll Most Likely Be Asked
11. Ant & Maven Interview Questions You'll Most Likely Be Asked
12. Apache Web Server Interview Questions You'll Most Likely Be Asked
13. Artificial Intelligence Interview Questions You'll Most Likely Be Asked
14. ASP.NET Interview Questions You'll Most Likely Be Asked
15. Automated Software Testing Interview Questions You'll Most Likely Be Asked
16. Base SAS Interview Questions You'll Most Likely Be Asked
17. BEA WebLogic Server Interview Questions You'll Most Likely Be Asked
18. C & C++ Interview Questions You'll Most Likely Be Asked
19. C# Interview Questions You'll Most Likely Be Asked
20. CCNA Interview Questions You'll Most Likely Be Asked
21. Cloud Computing Interview Questions You'll Most Likely Be Asked
22. Computer Architecture Interview Questions You'll Most Likely Be Asked
23. Computer Networks Interview Questions You'll Most Likely Be Asked
24. Core JAVA Interview Questions You'll Most Likely Be Asked
25. Data Structures & Algorithms Interview Questions You'll Most Likely Be Asked
26. EJB 3.0 Interview Questions You'll Most Likely Be Asked
27. Entity Framework Interview Questions You'll Most Likely Be Asked
28. Fedora & RHEL Interview Questions You'll Most Likely Be Asked
29. Hadoop BIG DATA Interview Questions You'll Most Likely Be Asked
30. Hibernate, Spring & Struts Interview Questions You'll Most Likely Be Asked
31. HR Interview Questions You'll Most Likely Be Asked
32. HTML, XHTML and CSS Interview Questions You'll Most Likely Be Asked
33. HTML5 Interview Questions You'll Most Likely Be Asked
34. IBM WebSphere Application Server Interview Questions You'll Most Likely Be Asked
35. iOS SDK Interview Questions You'll Most Likely Be Asked
36. Java / J2EE Design Patterns Interview Questions You'll Most Likely Be Asked
37. Java / J2EE Interview Questions You'll Most Likely Be Asked
38. JavaScript Interview Questions You'll Most Likely Be Asked
39. JavaServer Faces Interview Questions You'll Most Likely Be Asked
40. JDBC Interview Questions You'll Most Likely Be Asked
41. jQuery Interview Questions You'll Most Likely Be Asked
42. JSP-Servlet Interview Questions You'll Most Likely Be Asked
43. JUnit Interview Questions You'll Most Likely Be Asked
44. Linux Interview Questions You'll Most Likely Be Asked
45. Linux System Administrator Interview Questions You'll Most Likely Be Asked
46. Mac OS X Lion Interview Questions You'll Most Likely Be Asked
47. Mac OS X Snow Leopard Interview Questions You'll Most Likely Be Asked
48. Microsoft Access Interview Questions You'll Most Likely Be Asked
49. Microsoft Powerpoint Interview Questions You'll Most Likely Be Asked
50. Microsoft Word Interview Questions You'll Most Likely Be Asked
51. MySQL Interview Questions You'll Most Likely Be Asked

www.vibrantpublishers.com

52. Networking Interview Questions You'll Most Likely Be Asked
53. OOPS Interview Questions You'll Most Likely Be Asked
54. Operating Systems Interview Questions You'll Most Likely Be Asked
55. Oracle Database Administration Interview Questions You'll Most Likely Be Asked
56. Oracle E-Business Suite Interview Questions You'll Most Likely Be Asked
57. ORACLE PL/SQL Interview Questions You'll Most Likely Be Asked
58. Perl Programming Interview Questions You'll Most Likely Be Asked
59. PHP Interview Questions You'll Most Likely Be Asked
60. Python Interview Questions You'll Most Likely Be Asked
61. RESTful JAVA Web Services Interview Questions You'll Most Likely Be Asked
62. SAP HANA Interview Questions You'll Most Likely Be Asked
63. SAS Programming Guidelines Interview Questions You'll Most Likely Be Asked
64. Selenium Testing Tools Interview Questions You'll Most Likely Be Asked
65. Silverlight Interview Questions You'll Most Likely Be Asked
66. Software Repositories Interview Questions You'll Most Likely Be Asked
67. Software Testing Interview Questions You'll Most Likely Be Asked
68. SQL Server Interview Questions You'll Most Likely Be Asked
69. Tomcat Interview Questions You'll Most Likely Be Asked
70. UML Interview Questions You'll Most Likely Be Asked
71. Unix Interview Questions You'll Most Likely Be Asked
72. UNIX Shell Programming Interview Questions You'll Most Likely Be Asked
73. Windows Server 2008 R2 Interview Questions You'll Most Likely Be Asked
74. XLXP, XSLT, XPATH, XFORMS & XQuery Interview Questions You'll Most Likely Be Asked
75. XML Interview Questions You'll Most Likely Be Asked

For complete list visit
www.vibrantpublishers.com